MIGHTY MATHS

THIRD CLASS

MY PRACTICE BOOK

g GILL EDUCATION

MIGHTY MATHS

Contents

Practice	Page
Week 1	4
Week 2	6
Week 3	8
Week 4	10
Week 5	12
Week 6	14
Week 7	16
Week 8	18
Week 9	20
Week 10	22
Week 11	24
Week 12	26
Week 13	28
Week 14	30
Week 15	32
Week 16	34
Week 17	36
Week 18	38
Week 19	40
Week 20	42
Week 21	44
Week 22	46
Week 23	48
Week 24	50
Week 25	52
Week 26	54
Week 27	56
Week 28	58
Week 29	60
Week 30	62
Week 31	64
Week 32	66

Assessment	Page
Week 1	68
Week 2	68
Week 3	69
Week 4	69
Week 5	70
Week 6	70
Week 7	71
Week 8	71
Week 9	72
Week 10	72
Week 11	73
Week 12	73
Week 13	74
Week 14	74
Week 15	75
Week 16	75
Week 17	76
Week 18	76
Week 19	77
Week 20	77
Week 21	78
Week 22	78
Week 23	79
Week 24	79
Week 25	80
Week 26	80
Week 27	81
Week 28	81
Week 29	82
Week 30	82
Week 31	83
Week 32	83

Helpful Tools	84

The *Mighty Maths* Third Class Practice Book

· Provides structured daily Maths practice for Third Class
· Aligns with the *Mighty Maths* programme and Third Class Pupil's Book
· Progresses with the Pupil's Book so that all questions are achievable for the children
· Covers all the Learning Outcomes of the new Primary Maths Curriculum
· Revisits all the Strands and Strand Units (especially on Mondays) so that children get frequent exposure to the more difficult Strands and Strand Units of the curriculum
· Provides daily practice in mental Maths and problem-solving skills
· Provides a weekly assessment each Friday
· Full of engaging, child-friendly and cognitively challenging activities.

Please note:

The authors of the *Mighty Maths* programme suggest that the Practice Book is used **a week behind** the Pupil's Book to allow time for the Strand to be covered and to consolidate learning.

1. Total: _____

2. $(50 + 4) - 6 =$ _____

3. 4 ladybirds have _____ legs.

4. Fill in the missing numbers.

40, 44, _____, 52, _____, _____, 60

5. _____ o'clock.

6. A triangle has more sides than a rectangle.   True ☐   False ☐

7. How many corners altogether?

_____ corners

8. Fill in the correct symbol: < (less than), = (equal) or > (greater than).

☐

9. Tilly bought a packet of popcorn for €1.50. She paid with a €2 coin. How much change did she get? _____

10. Gordon had 53 marbles. He lost 10 and won 20 marbles in a game. How many marbles did he have at the end of the game? _____

Tuesday

1. What number is represented by the Dienes blocks?

Total:
_____

2. Show 467 on the abacus.

3. Use the correct symbol: < (less than), = (equal to) or > (greater than).

(a) 321 ☐ 516   (b) 412 ☐ 412

(c) 725 ☐ 752

4. Mark these numbers on the number line:

600   400   100   700   200   800

0   1,000

5. Record these numbers in digits.

(a) Two hundred and fifty-nine _____

(b) Five hundred and sixty-one _____

(c) Seven hundred and three _____

6. Record these numbers in expanded form on the the part-whole models.

7. How many hundreds (h), tens (t) and units (u) are in each of these numbers?

(a) 112 = ___ h ___ t ___ u

(b) 962 = ___ h ___ t ___ u

(c) 350 = ___ h ___ t ___ u

8. Order these numbers from lowest to highest value.

906   234   102   467   476

_____ _____ _____ _____ _____

9. Order these numbers from highest to lowest value.

480   134   283   691   619

_____ _____ _____ _____ _____

10. I am greater than 560 but less than 570. I have 5 units. I am _____.

Wednesday

1. What number is represented by the Dienes blocks?

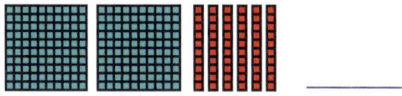 _____

2. Show 714 on the abacus.   h   t   u

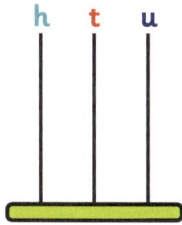

3. Use the correct symbol:
   < (less than), = (equal to)
   or > (greater than).
   (a) 615 ☐ 213   (b) 513 ☐ 729

4. Record these numbers in digits.
   (a) Six hundred and twenty-three

   _____

   (b) One hundred and ten _____

5. Record these numbers in digits.
   (a) Nine hundred and fifteen _____
   (b) Six hundred and sixty _____

6. Record these numbers in expanded form on the part-whole models.

7. (a) $500 + 60 + 2 =$ _____
   (b) $700 + 20 + 1 =$ _____

8. (a) 307 = ___ h ___ t ___ u
   (b) 629 = ___ h ___ t ___ u

9. Order these numbers from lowest to highest value.

   | 690 | 423 | 432 | 201 | 763 |

   _____ _____ _____ _____ _____

10. Order these numbers from highest to lowest value.

   | 322 | 314 | 840 | 916 | 804 |

   _____ _____ _____ _____ _____

Thursday

1. What number is represented by the Dienes blocks?

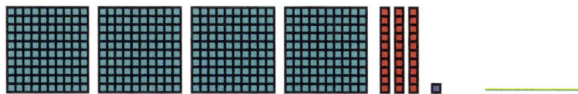 _____

2. Show 633 on the abacus.   h   t   u

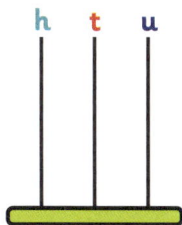

3. Write <, > or =.
   (a) 196 ☐ 312   (b) 872 ☐ 279

4. Record these numbers in digits.
   (a) Two hundred and sixty-one _____
   (b) Six hundred and nineteen _____

5. How many hundreds (h), tens (t) and units (u) in each of these numbers?
   (a) 919 = ___ h ___ t ___ u
   (b) 261 = ___ h ___ t ___ u

6. Record these numbers in their expanded form on the part-whole models.

7. (a) $600 + 50 + 4 =$ _____
   (b) $300 + 70 + 6 =$ _____

8. Record in digits.
   Three hundred and forty-seven _____

9. Order these numbers from lowest to highest value.

   | 690 | 423 | 432 | 201 | 763 |

   _____ _____ _____ _____ _____

10. Order these numbers from highest to lowest value.

   | 567 | 241 | 576 | 916 | 301 |

   _____ _____ _____ _____ _____

Monday | Look Back

1. Which number is represented by the Dienes blocks?

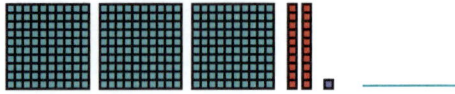 _____

2. Show 531 on the abacus.

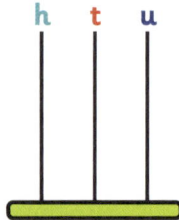

3. Ring the units/ones in each of these numbers.

   326   406   289   512   600

   417   756   833   111   999

4. Ring the tens in each of these numbers.

   129   345   617   209   522

   874   638   751   951   423

5. Record these numbers in their expanded form on the part-whole models.

6. Ring the hundreds in each of these numbers.

   690   213   458   347   501
   725   900   832   123   200

7. (a) $784 = $ ___ h ___ t ___ u

   (b) $563 = $ ___ h ___ t ___ u

   (c) $627 = $ ___ h ___ t ___ u

8. Record these numbers in digits.

   (a) Four hundred and seventeen

   _____

   (b) Three hundred and five _____

   (c) Eight hundred and eighty-eight

   _____

9. Order these numbers from lowest to highest value.

   | 617 | 458 | 312 | 542 | 321 |

   ___ ___ ___ ___ ___

10. Order these numbers from highest to lowest value.

    | 238 | 799 | 350 | 818 | 881 |

    ___ ___ ___ ___ ___

Tuesday

1. $243 + 112 = $ _____

2. $154 + 221 = $ _____

3. Round 73 to the nearest 10. ____

4. Jake has 235 marbles. He buys 143 more. How many does he have now? _____

5. Round 46 to the nearest 10. ____

6. Add 178 and 267. _____

7. Round 243 to the nearest 100. _____

8. $299 + 401 = $ _____

9. What is the sum of 513 and 289? _____

10. Round 678 to the nearest 100. _____

Wednesday

1. (a) 264 + 37 = _____

   (b) 482 + 398 = _____

   (c) 679 + 125 = _____

2. (a) What is the total of 503 and 191?

   _____

   (b) What is the total of 730 and 229?

   _____

3. Emma has 216 toy cars, her brother has 358 toy cars. How many toy cars do they have together? _____

4. A baker made 452 cupcakes in the morning and 329 in the afternoon. How many did he bake in total?

   _____

5. 725 + 188 = _____

6. 549 + 437 = _____

7. Emma counted 638 shells on the beach. Her friend counted 219. How many did they count in total?

   _____

8. 784 + 235 = _____

9. A train carries 465 passengers in the first coach and 372 in the second. How many passengers are in both coaches?

   _____

10. There are 899 people at a concert. 125 more arrive. How many are there now? _____

Thursday

1. 528 – 214 = _____

2. 376 – 153 = _____

3. 705 – 482 = _____

4. A shop had 672 chocolates. It sold 348. How many are left? _____

5. (a) 841 – 267 = _____

   (b) 491 – 287 = _____

   (c) 903 – 352 = _____

6. Liam had 362 points on a computer game. He then lost 145 points. How many points does he have left?

   _____

   POINTS: 362

7. Third Class collected 435 plastic bottles and cans for recycling. They recycled 218 plastic bottles. How many cans did they recycle? _____

8. Sarah had 512 stickers. She gave 275 to her friend. How many does she have left? _____

9. A school had 785 students. 324 students left. How many are there now? _____

10. (a) Subtract 429 from 600. _____

    (b) Subtract 459 from 938. _____

Monday | Look Back

1. Shade $\frac{1}{2}$ of this shape.

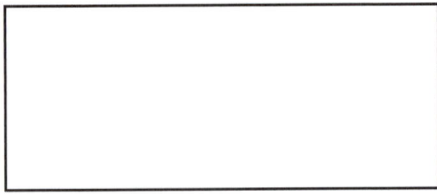

2. What is the value of the 7 in the number 374? ____

3. What time will it be 2 hours after 3:30 p.m.? _____

4. Ellie has €2. She buys a toy for €1.20. How much change does she get?

   _____

5. A watermelon weighs 2 kg. A bunch of bananas weigh 1 kg less. How much does the bunch of bananas weigh?

   _____

6. A bottle holds 1 litre of water. How many 500 ml cups can you fill from it?

   _____

7. Name a 3-D shape that can roll and has no edges.

   _____

8. A 2-D shape has 4 equal sides and 4 corners. What is it called?

   _____

9. Draw a triangle. Now flip (reflect) it. What does it look like?

10. Ben has 24 apples. He shares them equally between 4 friends. How many apples does each friend get?

    _____

Tuesday

1. Complete the repeated addition sentence. 2 + 2 + 2 + 2 = ___

2. 5 × 2 = ____

3. 9 × 2 = ____

4. 3 × 2 = ____

5. Write a multiplication sentence for 'Double seven'.

   _____

6. Lily has 4 baskets. Each basket has 2 apples. How many apples in total?

   ___ × ___ = ___

7. 6 × 2 = ____

8. James buys 8 packs of stickers. Each pack has 2 stickers. How many stickers does he have?

   ___ × ___ = ____

9. Continue the number pattern.

   2, 4, 6, 8, ____, ____, ____, ____, ____, ____, ____, ____

10. One crab has 8 legs. How many legs do 2 crabs have?

    ___ × ___ = ____

Wednesday

1. Complete the repeated addition sentence.

   $4 + 4 + 4 + 4 + 4 =$ ____

2. $2 \times 4 =$ ___

3. $4 \times 4 =$ ____

4. $7 \times 4 =$ ____

5. Write a multiplication sentence for 'Four times six'.

   _____

6. There are 3 shelves. Each shelf holds 4 books. How many books in total?

   __ $\times$ __ $=$ ____

7. A farmer has 10 cows. Each cow has 4 legs. How many legs in total?

   ____ $\times$ __ $=$ ____

8. Continue the number pattern.

   4, 8, 12, 16, ____, ____, ____, ____,

   ____, ____, ____, ____

9. Ella buys 9 boxes of cupcakes. Each box contains 4 cupcakes. How many cupcakes does she have in total?

   ___ $\times$ ___ $=$ ____

10. One chair has 4 legs. How many legs do 8 chairs have?

    ___ $\times$ ___ $=$ ____

Thursday

1. Complete the repeated addition sentence.

   $8 + 8 + 8 + 8 =$ ____

2. $2 \times 8 =$ ____

3. $3 \times 8 =$ ____

4. $7 \times 8 =$ ____

5. Write a multiplication sentence for 'Eight times five'.

   _____

6. A spider has 8 legs. How many legs do 3 spiders have?

   __ $\times$ __ $=$ ____

7. Continue the number pattern.

   8, 16, 24, 32, ____, ____, ____, ____,

   ____, ____, ____, ____, ____

8. A baker makes 8 cakes every day. How many cakes does she bake in 6 days?

   __ $\times$ __ $=$ ____

9. A tug-of-war team has 8 players. If there are 4 teams, how many players are there altogether?

   ___ $\times$ ___ $=$ ____

10. Jane has 8 bags. Each bag holds 8 apples. How many apples does she have in total?

    ___ $\times$ ___ $=$ ____

Monday   Look Back

1. You have a bag of 8 sweets. You eat $\frac{1}{2}$ of them. How many sweets did you eat? ___

2. Aoife collected data on pets in Third Class and recorded the data on a tally chart.

Dogs		IIII III
Cats		IIII
Rabbits		IIII III

(a) Which pet is the most popular?

_____

(b) How many pupils had a pet rabbit? ____

3. Liam has €10. He buys a book for €4.75. How much change would he get from €10?

_____

4. It is 3:00 p.m. now. What time will it be in 30 minutes? _____

5. A small box weighs 2 kg. A medium box weighs 1 kg more. How much does the medium box weigh? ___ kg

6. If you paint all the faces of a cube, how many faces would be painted? ___

7. Name a 3-D shape that has 6 faces, 12 edges and 8 corners.

_____

8. Draw a shape that has only 3 sides. What is it called? _____

9. 125 − 68 = ____

10. If ☐ + 7 = 15, ☐ = ___

Tuesday

1. (a) Draw the next 2 shapes in the pattern.

(b) Rule: _____

2. Draw the next 2 shapes in the pattern.

3. Draw the next 2 shapes in the pattern

4. Draw the next 2 shapes in the pattern.

5. Draw the next 3 shapes in the pattern.

6. Draw the next 2 shapes in the pattern

7. Draw the next 2 shapes in the pattern.

8. Draw the next 3 shapes in the pattern.

9. Draw the next 4 shapes in the pattern.

10. Draw the next 4 shapes in the pattern.

Wednesday

1. Draw the next 3 shapes in the pattern.

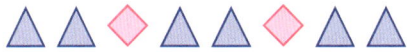

△ △ ◇ △ △ ◇ △ △

2. Continue the pattern. Then, write the rule.

2, 6, 12, 20, ____, ____, ____

Rule: _____

3. Continue the pattern. Then, write the rule.

100, 90, 80, ____, ____, ____

Rule: _____

4. Continue the pattern. Then, write the rule.

1, 3, 6, 10, 15, ____, ____

Rule: _____

5. Continue the pattern. Then, write the rule.

4, 7, 11, 16, 22, ____, ____, ____

Rule: _____

6. Continue the pattern. Then, write the rule.

2, 5, 10, 17, 26, ____, ____

Rule: _____

7. Continue the decreasing pattern. Then, write the rule.

100, 95, 90, 85, ____, ____, ____

Rule: _____

8. Continue the pattern. Then, write the rule.

2, 4, 8, 16, ____, ____, ____

Rule: _____

9. Continue the pattern.

3, 6, 9, 12, ____, ____, ____

10. Draw the next 2 shapes.

▽ △ △ ▽ △ △ ▽ △ △

Thursday

1. $4 \times 3 = 12$, so $12 \div 3 =$ ___

2. $5 \times 6 = 30$, so $30 \div 5 =$ ___

3. $8 \times 7 = 56$, so $56 \div 8 =$ ___

4. $6 \times 4 = 24$, so $24 \div 6 =$ ___

5. $9 \times 4 = 36$, so $36 \div 4 =$ ___

6. Fill in the missing numbers.

  (a) $4 \times 2 = 8$ **(b)** $20 \div 4 = 5$

      $8 \div 2 =$ ___ $5 \times 4 =$ ___

7. $7 \times 6 = 42$, so $42 \div 6 =$ ___

8. $3 \times 5 = 15$, so $15 \div 5 =$ ___

9. Continue the number pattern.

6, 12, 18, ____, ____, ____

Rule: _____

10. **(a)** $8 \times 3 = 24$, so $24 \div 3 =$ ___

  (b) $10 \times 4 = 40$, so $40 \div 4 =$ ___

  (c) $9 \times 7 = 63$, so $63 \div 7 =$ ___

Monday | Look Back

1. There are 16 strawberries in a punnet. You eat $\frac{1}{4}$ of them. How many strawberries did you eat?

   _____

2. This bar chart shows the number of Third Class pupils who walk, cycle or take the bus to school.

   How many pupils were surveyed?

   _____

3. Draw hands on the clock to show 7:15.

4. Ben has €5. He buys a sandwich for €3.25. How much money does he have left? _____

5. Two textbooks weigh 3 kg. Two notebooks weigh 2 kg less. How much do the 2 notebooks weigh? _____

6. A piece of string is 1 metre long. You cut off 40 cm. How long is the piece that is left? _____ cm

7. Name a 3-D shape that has 2 circular faces and 1 curved surface.

   _____

8. Draw a shape that has two lines of symmetry.

9. Move the pink square one square to the right. Draw it.

10. (a) $7 \times 2 =$ _____

    (b) $5 \times 4 =$ _____

    (c) $3 \times 8 =$ _____

Tuesday

1. Subtract 2 repeatedly until you reach 0.

   16 – ____ – ____ – ____ – ___ – ___ – ___ – ___ – ___

   How many times did you subtract? ___

2. Subtract 2 repeatedly until you reach 0.

   10 – ___ – ___ – ___ – ___ – ___

   How many times did you subtract? ___

3. Aoife has 14 sweets. She shares them equally between herself and her friend. How many sweets do they get each? ___

4. $8 \div 2 =$ _____   5. $12 \div 2 =$ _____

6. $20 \div 2 =$ _____   7. $18 \div 2 =$ _____

8. A farmer has 10 apples and wants to put them into 2 equal baskets. How many apples are in each basket? ___

9. There are 16 balloons at a party. Each guest gets 2 balloons. How many guests were at the party? ___

10. A rope is 12 metres long. If you cut it into pieces of 2 metres each, how many pieces would there be? _____

Wednesday

1. Subtract 4 repeatedly until you reach 0.

   20 – ___ – ___ – ___ – ___ – ___

   How many times did you subtract? ___

2. Subtract 4 repeatedly until you reach 0.

   12 – ___ – ___ – ___

   How many times did you subtract? ___

3. $16 \div 4 =$ ___

4. $8 \div 4 =$ ___

5. $24 \div 4 =$ ___

6. $32 \div 4 =$ ___

7. Dad needs to bake 28 pies. Each baking tray holds 4 pies. How many trays does he need? ___

8. Sophie has 20 pens. She sorts them into piles of 4. How many piles does she make?

   ___

9. A basket holds 4 pears. How many baskets do you need for 12 pears?

   ___

10. A teacher has 24 stickers and divides them equally among 4 students. How many stickers does each student get?

    ___

Thursday

1. Subtract 8 repeatedly until you reach 0.

   32 – ___ – ___ – ___ – ___

   How many times did you subtract? ___

2. Subtract 8 repeatedly until you reach 0.

   24 – ___ – ___ – ___

   How many times did you subtract? ___

3. $16 \div 8 =$ ___

4. $40 \div 8 =$ ___

5. $8 \div 8 =$ ___

6. $56 \div 8 =$ ___

7. One shelf holds 8 books. How many shelves are needed for 32 books? ___

8. A farmer has 48 oranges. She packs them into baskets of 8. How many baskets does she need? ___

9. 16 students are seated equally in rows of 8. How many rows are there? ___

10. A baker made 64 cookies and put them into boxes of 8. How many boxes are there? ___

Monday — Look Back

1. What is the value of the 5 in the number 352? ____

2. A chocolate bar is broken into 4 equal pieces. Sam ate 1 piece. What fraction of the chocolate bar did she eat? $\frac{\square}{\square}$

3. Look at this pictogram showing the number of ice creams sold in one week.

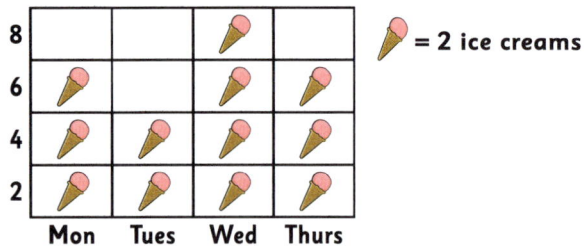

= 2 ice creams

How many ice creams were sold on Wednesday? _____

4. Draw hands on the analogue clock to show 2:45.

5. Ms Lynch travels 30 km from her home to school. After 15 km, she stops for petrol. How much further does she have left to travel? ____

6. Which 3-D shape has 1 curved surface and no edges?
_____

7. A cinema ticket costs €12. How much would 4 tickets cost? €____

8. Draw a shape with 2 lines of symmetry.

9. $\square$ – 9 = 15, $\square$ = ____

10. (a) 9 × 2 = ____   (b) 6 × 4 = ____
(c) 5 × 8 = ____

Tuesday

1. Draw the next 2 shapes in the pattern.

2. Continue the number pattern and write the rule.
332, 338, 344, 350, _____, _____
Rule: _____

3. Continue the number pattern and write the rule.
167, 163, 159, 155, _____, _____
Rule: _____

4. Continue the number pattern and write the rule.
320, 310, 300, 290, _____, _____
Rule: _____

5. Continue the number pattern and write the rule.
536, 542, 548, 554, _____, _____
Rule: _____

6. 8 friends are going to a concert. Each friend buys ___ tickets. 32 tickets were bought in total.

7. At a bake sale, there were ____ trays of cookies. Each tray has 6 cookies. There were 60 cookies in total.

8. Nancy planted 35 flowers in 5 rows. Each row had ___ flowers.

9. Tomás shared 48 marbles equally among 4 friends. He gave ___ marbles to each friend.

10. 80 students are going on a school trip. One bus has 20 seats. How many buses are needed so all students have a seat? ___

Wednesday

1. Fill in the missing numbers.
   245, 255, 265, _____, 275, _____
   What is the rule?
   _____

2. Draw the next 2 shapes.
   ○ ▢ ○ ▢ ○ ▢ ○ ▢ ○
   What is the rule?
   _____

3. What are the next 2 numbers?
   996, 984, 972, 960, _____, _____
   What is the rule?
   _____

4. What are the next 2 numbers?
   380, 390, 400, 410, _____, _____

5. Continue the number pattern and write the rule.
   724, 732, 740, 748, _____, _____
   Rule: _____

6. At a talent show, 7 teams participated. There were 42 performers in total. Each team had ___ performers.

7. Maria sells books at the bookshop. She sells the same number of books each day for 8 days. She sells 40 books in total. How many books does she sell per day? ___

8. Emily buys 3 packs of cards. Each pack has ___ cards. She bought 27 cards in total.

9. There are ___ boxes of cookies. Each box has 6 cookies. There are 72 cookies in total.

10. A farmer collects 10 eggs every day. After ___ days, he has 50 eggs.

Thursday

1. What are the next 2 numbers?
   316, 310, 304, 298, _____, _____
   What is the rule?
   _____

2. Draw the next 2 shapes.
   ▢ ◇ ▢ ◇ ▢ ▢ ◇ ▢ ◇ ▢ ◇ ▢

3. What are the next 2 numbers?
   500, 480, 460, 440, _____, _____
   What is the rule?
   _____

4. What are the next 2 numbers?
   625, 630, 635, 640, _____, _____
   What is the rule?
   _____

5. What are the next 2 numbers?
   218, 224, 230, 236, _____, _____
   What is the rule?
   _____

6. In a basketball tournament, ___ teams played. Each team had 5 players. 60 players participated in the tournament.

7. A teacher gives 2 pencils to each student. He gives out 40 pencils in total, so there are _____ students in his class.

8. A farmer has 16 baskets. Each basket holds 3 plums. How many plums does the farmer have in total? _____

9. A factory has 7 boxes of yo-yos. How many does each box hold if there are 56 yo-yos altogether? ___

10. 12 runners run a total of 36 laps. If they run the same number of laps each, how many laps does each runner run? ___

Monday | Look Back

1. Draw hands on the analogue clock to show 6:30.

2. Sarah has 453 marbles. Her friend gives her 287 more. How many marbles does Sarah have now?

   _____

3. What is the value of the 4 in the number 472? _____

4. (a) 8 × 2 = _____   (b) 6 × 4 = _____
   (c) 10 × 8 = _____

5. There are 4 colouring pencils in each cup. If you have 5 cups, how many pencils do you have in total? _____

6. Divide 16 by 2. ___

7. Divide 32 by 4. ___

8. 6 + ▢ = 13, ▢ = ___

9. A stick is 150 cm long. You cut off 45 cm. How long is the stick now?

   _____

10. You have €6.80. You buy a toy for €2.50. How much money do you have left? _____

Tuesday

1. Colour half of this set.

2. Shade $\frac{1}{4}$ of this rectangle.

3. Which fraction is missing?

   $\frac{1}{4}$, $\frac{\square}{\square}$, $\frac{3}{4}$, $\frac{4}{4}$

4. Which fraction is not shown on the number line?

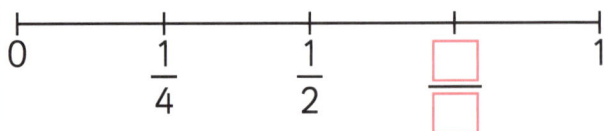

   0 ——— $\frac{1}{4}$ ——— $\frac{1}{2}$ ——— $\frac{\square}{\square}$ ——— 1

5. Write an equivalent fraction for

   $\frac{1}{2} = \frac{\square}{4}$

6. If a line is divided into 4 equal parts and 1 part is shaded, what fraction of the line is shaded? $\frac{\square}{\square}$

7. Lily has 8 sweets. She gives $\frac{1}{4}$ of them to her friend. How many does she give away?

   _____

8. Which is greater: $\frac{1}{2}$ or $\frac{1}{4}$? $\frac{\square}{\square}$

   Explain why.

   _____

9. A pizza is cut into 4 slices. You eat 2 slices. What fraction of the pizza is left?

   $\frac{\square}{\square}$

10. Colour in $\frac{2}{4}$ of this shape.

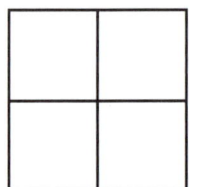

Wednesday

1. Ring $\frac{1}{8}$ of this set.

2. Write the missing fraction.

$$0, \frac{1}{8}, \frac{\square}{\square}, \frac{3}{8}$$

3. Shade $\frac{4}{8}$ of this rectangle.

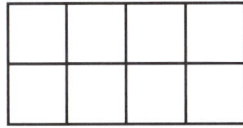

4. Write an equivalent fraction for $\frac{4}{8}$. $\frac{\square}{4}$

5. If one part is $\frac{1}{8}$, how many equal parts make up the whole? ___

6. Chloe has 16 stickers. She gives away $\frac{1}{8}$ of them. How many does she give away? ___

7. An orange is cut into 8 pieces. You eat 3. What fraction is left? $\frac{\square}{\square}$

8. $\frac{1}{2} = \frac{4}{8}$

True $\square$ False $\square$

9. Which fraction is greater: $\frac{1}{8}$ or $\frac{1}{4}$? $\frac{\square}{\square}$ Explain why.

_____

10. Draw a number line and place the following fractions.

0    $\frac{1}{8}$ $\frac{1}{4}$ $\frac{3}{8}$ $\frac{1}{2}$

Thursday

1. Colour $\frac{1}{3}$ of this set:

2. Write the missing fraction.

$$\frac{1}{6}, \frac{1}{3}, \frac{\square}{\square}, \frac{2}{3}, \frac{5}{6}, 1$$

3. Shade $\frac{2}{6}$ of this rectangle.

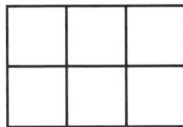

4. Write an equivalent fraction to $\frac{2}{6}$. $\frac{\square}{3}$

5. One part = $\frac{1}{3}$. What fraction makes up the whole? $\frac{\square}{\square}$

6. Tom has 18 marbles. He gives away $\frac{1}{3}$ of them. How many does he give away? ___

7. A block of cheese is cut into 6 equal slices. 4 slices are used for sandwiches.

What fraction is left? $\frac{\square}{\square}$

8. Which is greater: $\frac{1}{3}$ or $\frac{1}{6}$? $\frac{\square}{\square}$ Explain why.

_____

9. $\frac{2}{6} = \frac{1}{3}$

True $\square$ False $\square$

10. Draw a number line and place the following fractions.

0    $\frac{1}{6}$ $\frac{1}{3}$ $\frac{3}{6}$ $\frac{2}{3}$ 1

Monday — Look Back

1. How many days are in 3 weeks?

   _____

2. You have €5.75. You buy a toy for €2.50. How much money do you have left? _____

3. What is the value of the 2 in the number 962? ___

4. Divide 32 by 4. ___

5. A line is divided into 6 equal parts. What fraction of the line is 1 part? $\frac{\Box}{\Box}$

6. Oisín's long jump record is 120 cm. Sam's is 40 cm less than Oisín's. What is Sam's long jump record?

   _____

7. Draw a rectangle and mark the lines of symmetry.

8. $11 \times 8 =$ ____

9. How many months are there in a year?

   _____

10. A cake is cut into 6 equal parts. You and a friend eat 1 part each. What fraction of the cake is left? $\frac{\Box}{\Box}$

Tuesday

1. Colour $\frac{3}{9}$ of the fraction wheel.

2. Write the correct symbol: <, > or =.
   $\frac{2}{9} \,\Box\, \frac{1}{3}$

3. What fractions are missing on the number line?

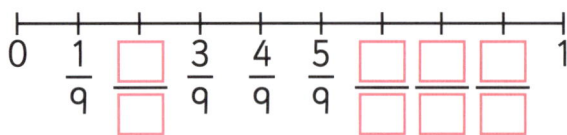

   0   $\frac{1}{9}$ $\frac{\Box}{\Box}$ $\frac{3}{9}$ $\frac{4}{9}$ $\frac{5}{9}$ $\frac{\Box}{\Box}$ $\frac{\Box}{\Box}$ $\frac{\Box}{\Box}$ 1

4. $\frac{3}{9} = \frac{1}{\Box}$

5. $\frac{2}{9} + \frac{4}{9} = \frac{\Box}{\Box}$

6. $\frac{7}{9} - \frac{3}{9} = \frac{\Box}{\Box}$

7. Which is greater: $\frac{5}{9}$ or $\frac{2}{3}$? $\frac{\Box}{\Box}$ How do you know?

   _____

8. A chocolate bar is divided into 9 equal pieces. You eat 4 pieces. What fraction is left? $\frac{\Box}{\Box}$

9. A school has 90 students. $\frac{1}{9}$ of them play soccer. How many students play soccer? _____

10. A baker makes 9 loaves of bread. He sells $\frac{5}{9}$ of them.

    (a) How many loaves does he sell? _____

    (b) How many are left? _____

Wednesday

1. Colour $\frac{2}{5}$ of the fraction wheel.

2. Write the correct symbol: <, > or =.

$\frac{3}{5}$ ☐ $\frac{4}{5}$

3. Which fraction is missing from the number line?

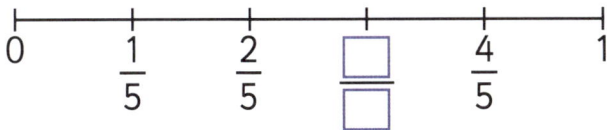

```
├────┼────┼────┼────┼────┤
0    1    2    ☐    4    1
     5    5    ☐    5
```

4. $\frac{1}{5} + \frac{2}{5} = \frac{\square}{\square}$

5. $\frac{4}{5} - \frac{2}{5} = \frac{\square}{\square}$

6. A pizza is cut into 5 slices.
3 slices have pepperoni.
What fraction has no pepperoni? $\frac{\square}{\square}$

7. A fruit bowl has 20 red and green grapes. $\frac{1}{5}$ of them are red. How many red grapes are there? _____

8. Which is greater: $\frac{3}{5}$ or $\frac{2}{5}$? $\frac{\square}{\square}$
How do you know?

_____

9. In a class of 25 students, $\frac{2}{5}$ are wearing blue jumpers. How many students are wearing blue jumpers? _____

10. A toy shop has 50 whistles in stock. It sells $\frac{3}{5}$ of them. How many whistles does it sell? _____
How many whistles does he have left?

_____

Thursday

1. Colour $\frac{4}{10}$ of the fraction wheel.

2. Write the correct symbol: <, > or =.

$\frac{4}{10}$ ☐ $\frac{4}{5}$

3. Which fractions are missing from the number line?

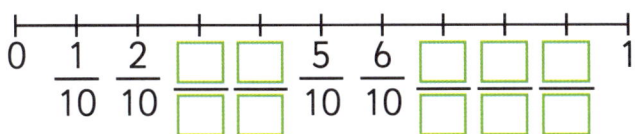

```
├──┼──┼──┼──┼──┼──┼──┼──┼──┼──┤
0  1  2  ☐  ☐  5  6  ☐  ☐  ☐  1
   10 10 ☐  ☐  10 10 ☐  ☐  ☐
```

4. $\frac{3}{10} + \frac{5}{10} = \frac{\square}{\square}$

5. $\frac{8}{10} - \frac{4}{10} = \frac{\square}{\square}$

6. Which is greater: $\frac{3}{5}$ or $\frac{4}{10}$? $\frac{\square}{\square}$
How do you know?

_____

7. Liam has 10 stickers. He gives $\frac{2}{10}$ to his friend and $\frac{3}{10}$ to his sister.
What fraction does he have left? $\frac{\square}{\square}$

8. A school has 100 students. $\frac{1}{10}$ of them walk to school. How many students walk to school? _____

9. A farmer has 40 cows. $\frac{2}{10}$ of them are brown. How many brown cows are there? _____

10. A book has 120 pages. Sam reads $\frac{3}{10}$ of the book on Monday and $\frac{2}{10}$ on Tuesday.

(a) How many pages has he read in total? _____

(b) How many pages are left? _____

Monday   Look Back

1.
```
  6 7 4
+ 2 6 2
```
[   ]

2. Which county won the most medals?

_____

County	Medals
Donegal	117
Galway	126
Carlow	203

3. Which county won the fewest medals?

_____

4. Will this shape tessellate?

Yes [ ]   No [ ]

5. Sally woke up at 6:00 a.m. Draw this time on the analogue clock.

6. Simon arrived home at 7:30 p.m. Draw this time on the analogue clock.

7. How much money do I have if I have 4 of these coins?

_____ c

8. How much?

_____ c

9. 18 ÷ 3 = _____

10. Write this number in digits: two hundred and eighteen _____

Tuesday

1. 1 metre (m) = _____ centimetres (cm)

2. Use a ruler to measure the length of the blue line below. _____ cm

3. Use a ruler to draw a line 8 cm long.

[   ]

4. Write the correct symbol: <, = or >.

115 cm [ ] 105 cm

5. (a) Estimate the length of this eraser.
_____ cm

(b) Use a ruler to find its actual length.
_____ cm

6. The string is _____ cm long.

7. 2 m 16 cm = _____ cm

8. 166 cm = ___ m _____ cm

9. The total height of the two flowers is _____ cm.

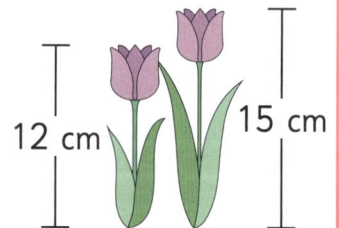

12 cm   15 cm

10. Calculate the total.

```
  m  cm
  1  27
+ 1  50
```
[   ]

Wednesday

1. There are _____ centimetres (cm) in 1 metre (m).

2. $\frac{1}{2}$ m = _____ cm

3. $\frac{1}{4}$ m = _____ cm

4. Fill in the correct symbol: <, = or >.

   90 cm ☐ 119 cm

5. Use a ruler to measure and record the length of the red line. _____ cm

   _____

6. Use a ruler to draw a line 6 cm long.

7. 1 m 90 cm = _____ cm

8. 306 cm = ___ m _____ cm

9. (a) Estimate the length of this sharpener. ___ cm

   (b) Using a ruler, find its actual length. ___ cm

10. How much longer is the green rope than the black rope?

    ___ m _____ cm

    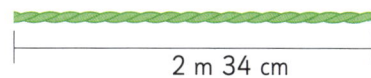

    2 m 34 cm

    1 m 12 cm

Thursday

1. There are _____ cm in $\frac{1}{4}$ m.

2. 2 m is the same as _____ cm.

3. The pen below is _____ cm long.

   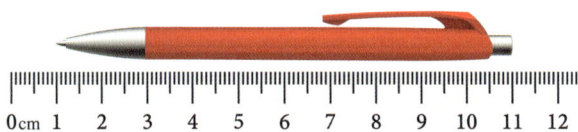

4. Use a ruler to measure and record the length of the purple line. _____ cm

   _____

5. Use a ruler to draw a line 7 cm long.

6. Fill in the correct symbol: <, = or >.

   1 m 85 cm ☐ 185 cm

7. 3 m 65 cm = _____ cm

8. 271 cm = ___ m _____ cm

9. Calculate the total length.

m	cm
3	56
+ 2	37

10. Calculate the difference between these two lengths.

m	cm
7	23
– 5	18

Monday | Look Back

1. Show 708 on the abacus.

   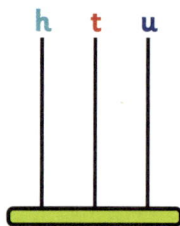

2.
```
   5 6 2
 + 3 8 4
 ───────
```

3. How many legs would 4 dogs have?

   ___ × ___ = ___

4. Draw any lines of symmetry on the square.

5. A concert started at half past 8 and finished two hours later. Draw the finish time on the clock.

6. $\frac{1}{2}$ an hour after 7:45 is [   ] : [   ]

7. $\frac{1}{4}$ litre of yoghurt costs 40c. How much for 1 litre? €___.___

8. Bob found this much money in his pocket. How much did he have? ___c

9. Draw the other half of the butterfly.

10. January has ___ days.

Tuesday

Work out the area of each rectangle.

1.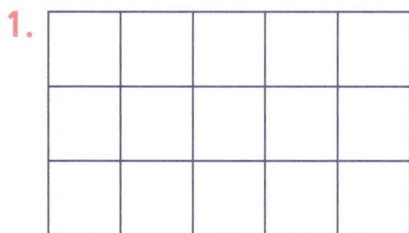

   Area = ___ cm²

2.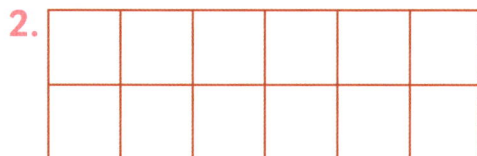

   Area = ___ cm²

3.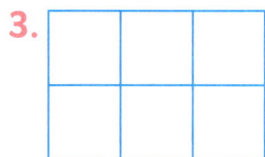

   Area = ___ cm²

4.

   Area = ___ cm²

5.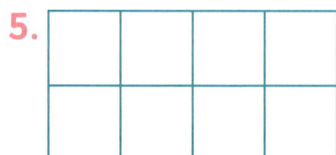

   Area = ___ cm²

6.  Area = ___ cm²

7. What would be the area of a rectangle double the size of the one in question 6? Area = ___ cm²

8. A shape has an area of 6 cm². Show what it could look like in the grid.

   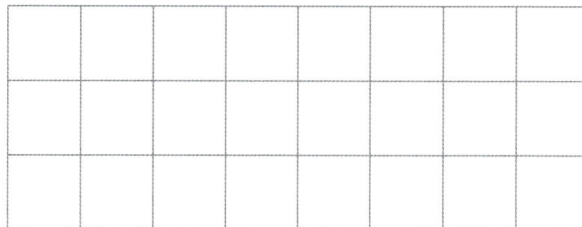

9. Find the total area of these 2 shapes.

   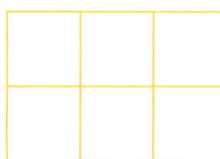 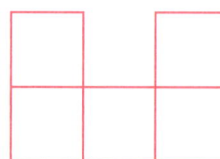

   Area = ___ cm²

10. Colour these shapes on the grid, then record the total area.

     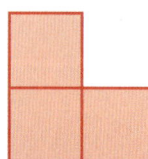 

    Area = ___ cm²

Wednesday

1. This shape has an area of _____ cm².

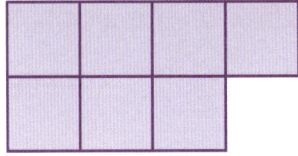

 A   B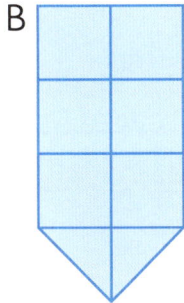

2. Area of shape A = _____ cm²

3. Area of B = _____ cm²

4. 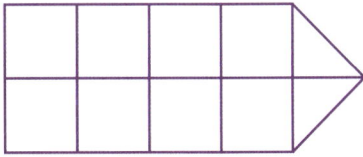   Area = _____ cm²

5. 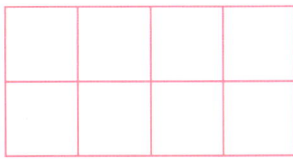   Area = _____ cm²

6.    Area = _____ cm²

7.

Area = _____ cm²

8. A shape has an area of 5 cm². Show what it could look like in the grid.

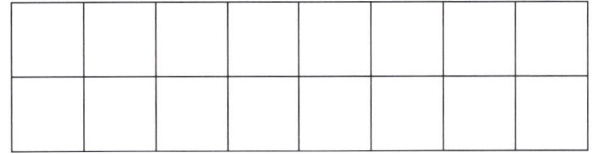

9. Find the total area of these 2 shapes.

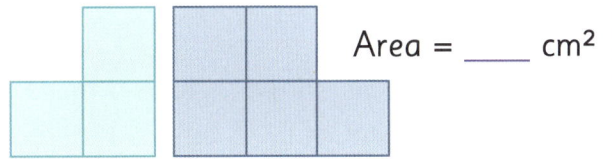   Area = _____ cm²

10. Colour these shapes on the grid, then record the area.

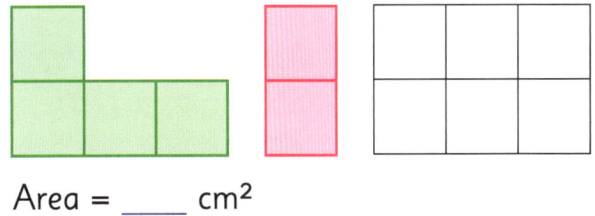

Area = _____ cm²

Thursday

1. This shape has an area of _____ cm².

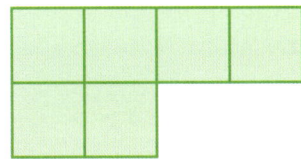

2. Area of shape A = _____ cm²

3. Area shape B = _____ cm²

A    B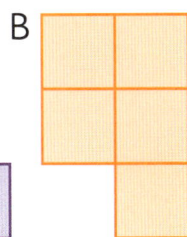

4. 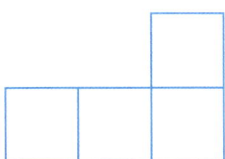   Area = _____ cm²

5.    Area = _____ cm²

6. 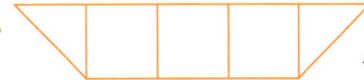   Area = _____ cm²

7.    Area = _____ cm²

8. Draw a shape with an area of 7 cm².

9. Colour these 2 shapes on the blank grid.

10. What is the total area of the shapes in question 9? Area = _____ cm²

Monday | Look Back

1. Draw lines to divide this rectangle into thirds.

2. What fraction of this shape is coloured in? ____

3. Name these 3-D objects.

_____ _____ _____

4. (a) Guess the shape: I have 6 faces, 8 corners and 12 edges. I have all square faces. I am a _____.

   (b) I have 3 faces, no vertices and 2 edges. I am a _____.

5. Draw a shape with an area of 4 cm².

6. Measure this string with a ruler and record the length. ____ cm.

Look at the graph and answer the questions.

Favourite Fruit

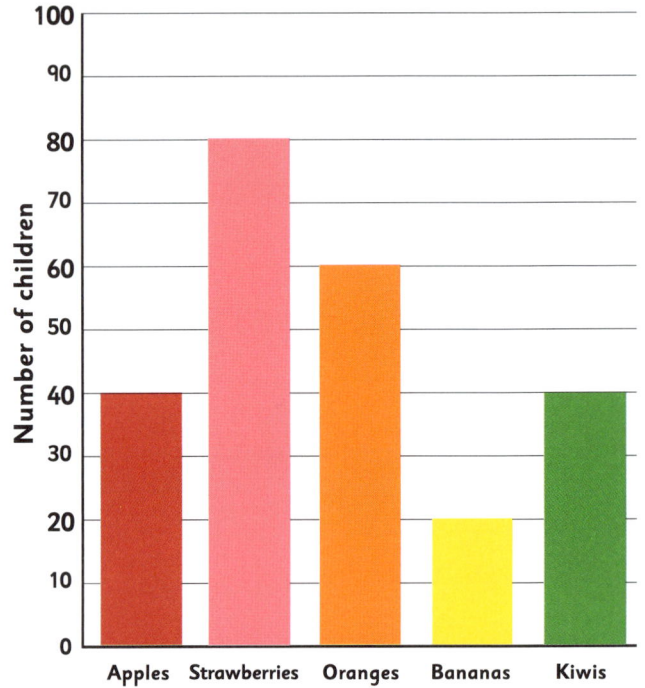

Number of children

Apples Strawberries Oranges Bananas Kiwis

7. How many children voted altogether? ____

8. How many voted for kiwis? ____

9. Which fruit got the fewest votes? _____

10. How many more children voted for oranges than bananas? ____

Tuesday

1. Colour $\frac{1}{10}$ of this shape.

2. Colour $\frac{3}{10}$ of this shape.

3. (a) Colour $\frac{6}{10}$ of this shape.

   (b) Write $\frac{6}{10}$ as a decimal fraction. _____

4. Write the number of raised fingers and thumbs as a decimal fraction. _____

5. What decimal fraction of this shape is coloured? _____

6. Colour 0.5 of this shape.

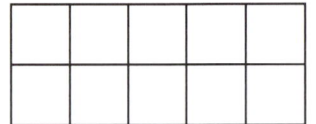

7. Write $\frac{9}{10}$ as a decimal fraction. _____

8. Write $\frac{10}{10}$ as a decimal fraction. _____

9. Fill in the missing decimal fractions.

0.3   0.8   1.0

10. Ring the decimal fraction with the greatest value.

    0.6   0.3   0.8   0.9

24   Week 11

Wednesday

1. (a) Colour $\frac{8}{10}$ of this shape.
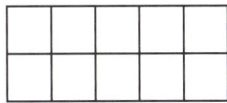

(b) Write $\frac{8}{10}$ as a decimal fraction. _____

2. (a) Colour $\frac{5}{10}$ of the shape.
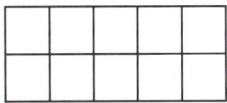

(b) Write $\frac{5}{10}$ as a decimal fraction. _____

3. (a) Colour $\frac{9}{10}$ of this shape.
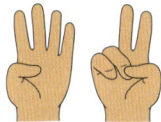

(b) Write $\frac{9}{10}$ as a decimal fraction. _____

4. Write the number of raised fingers as a decimal fraction. _____

5. What decimal fraction of this shape is coloured? _____
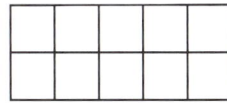

6. Colour 0.7 of this shape.

7. Write $\frac{1}{10}$ as a decimal fraction. _____

8. Write $\frac{2}{10}$ as a decimal fraction. _____

9. Fill in the missing decimal fractions.
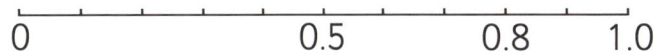
0   0.5   0.8   1.0

10. Ring the decimal fraction with the smallest value.

0.8   0.2   0.7   0.5

Thursday

1. Write as decimal fractions.

(a) Orange = _____

(b) White = _____
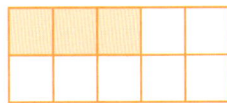

2. Write as decimal fractions.

(a) Red = _____

(b) Green = _____

(c) White = _____

3. Colour these decimal values.

(a) Blue = 0.2

(b) Yellow = 0.6

(c) Red = 0.2
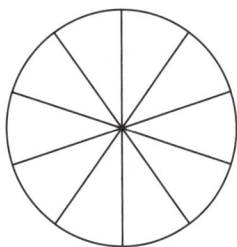

4. Colour 1.7.
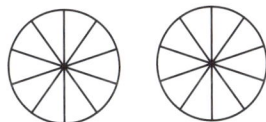

5. Colour 2.3.

6. Colour 3.6.
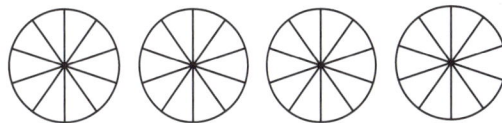

7. What decimal fraction is coloured?

_____
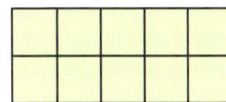 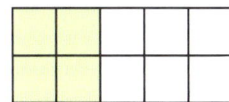

8. Ring the decimal fraction with the greatest value.

1.6   1.1   1.4   1.7

9. Ring the decimal fraction with the lowest value.

1.8   1.3   1.9   1.5

10. Show these values on the number line: 0.4, 0.7, 1.2, 1.6, 1.9.

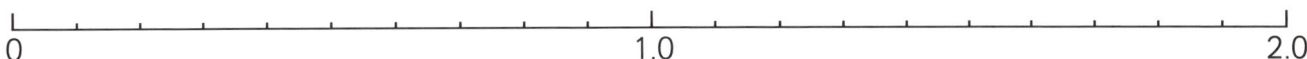
0   1.0   2.0

Monday | Look Back

1. What fraction of the shape is coloured? _____

2. There were 208 people at the pool on Tuesday. 316 people were there on Wednesday. How many people were there altogether on both days? _____

3. Michael had 432 marbles. Meg had 167 less than Michael. How many marbles did Meg have? _____

4. $36 \div 4 =$ ____

5. Use a ruler to draw a line 5 cm long.

6. Write the correct symbol: <, = or >.

902 ☐ 436

7. I had 24c. I shared half of my money with my cousin. I had _____c left.

8. Write this time in digital format and in words.

:

_____ past _____

9. Ring the weight that would be the heaviest to lift.

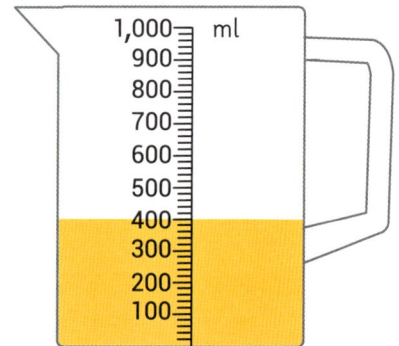

10 kg   30 kg   13 kg

10. How many ml of juice is in the jug?

_____ ml

1,000 ml
900
800
700
600
500
400
300
200
100

Tuesday

1. Round each decimal number to the nearest whole number.

(a) 2.3 ➔ ____   (b) 3.1 ➔ ____

(c) 7.5 ➔ ____   (d) 6.9 ➔ ____

(e) 4.7 ➔ ____   (f) 1.4 ➔ ____

2. Ben filled his bottle with 1.4 litres of water. Sarah filled her bottle with 1.9 litres of water. How much water do they have altogether? ____ litres

3. Sophie's ribbon is 2.5 metres long, and Jake's ribbon is 3.2 metres long.

(a) Whose ribbon is longer?

_____

(b) By how much? _____ m

4. A loaf of bread weighs 0.6 kg, and a bag of apples weighs 1.2 kg. What is the total weight of both items? ____ kg

5. $5.1 + 4.3 =$ _____

6. $6.2 + 1.3 =$ _____

7. $3.8 + 2.1 =$ _____

8. $7.6 + 1.3 =$ _____

9. $8.1 + 1.7 =$ _____

10. Write in the correct symbol: <, = or >.

5.8 ☐ 5.6

Wednesday

1. Round each decimal number to the nearest whole number.

    (a) 3.6 → ____   (b) 4.5 → ____

    (c) 5.2 → ____   (d) 5.8 → ____

2. Write the correct symbol: <, = or >.

    (a) 2.8 ☐ 3.1   (b) 6.6 ☐ 7.7

    (c) 1.7 ☐ 1.2   (d) 3.9 ☐ 3.9

3. 7.3 + 0.5 = _____

4. 8.5 + 4.3 = _____

5. 9.6 – 3.4 = _____

6. 5.9 – 4.5 = _____

7. Liam poured 0.6 litres of juice into his glass, and Ava poured 0.8 litres into hers.

    (a) Who has more juice?

    _____

    (b) By how much? ____ litres

8. Emma's pencil measures 4.7 cm. Round this to the nearest whole number.

    _____ cm

9. A watermelon weighs 2.3 kg. Round this weight to the nearest whole kilogram.
    ____ kg

10. Liam ran a race in 9.8 seconds. Round his time to the nearest whole second.

    ____ s

Thursday

1. Ring the number in which 3 has the lower value.

    3.2   6.3

2. Ring the number in which 5 has the greater value.

    17.5   15.2

3. Write the correct symbol: <, = or >.

    (a) 4.1 ☐ 4.7

    (b) 5.1 ☐ 0.5

4. 2.6 + 1.8 + 2.4 = _____

5. 3.2 + 2.5 + 0.7 = _____

6. 10.4 – 3.7 = _____

7. 9.2 – 5.3 = _____

8. Order the numbers from lowest to highest value.

    1.0   0.3   0.1   6.0   4.2   11.1   5.0   0.5

    ____ ____ ____ ____ ____ ____

    ____ ____

9. 0.1 is the same as $\frac{10}{10}$.

    True ☐   False ☐

10. Show these decimal fractions on the number lines.

    (a) 1.2, 1.5, 1.7, 1.9

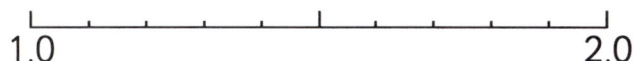

    (b) 2.1, 2.3, 2.6, 2.8

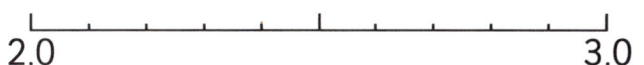

Monday — Look Back

1.
m	cm
15	26
+ 14	33

2. Colour 0.7.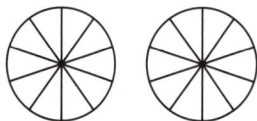

3. Divide 36 by 4. ___

4. A shape is divided into 6 equal parts. 1 part is shaded. What fraction of the shape is shaded? ▢/▢

5. Colour 1.2.

6. Divide 72 by 8. ___

7. 3.4 + 2.5 =

_____

8. Elle had €6.50. She found €2.75 in her pocket. How much money does she have now? _____

9. You have 845 trading cards. You give 378 cards to your friend. How many cards do you have left? _____

10. Continue the pattern.

Tuesday

Favourite Fruit	Number of Students
Apples	60
Bananas	40
Grapes	30 more than bananas
Oranges	Same as apples

1. Use the data from the table to complete the bar chart.

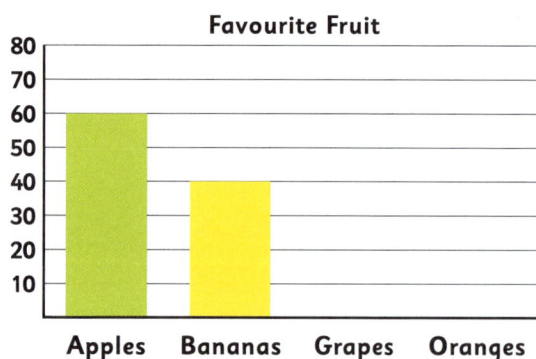

Favourite Fruit

2. Which fruit is the most popular?

_____

3. How many more students like apples than bananas? _____

4. Which 2 fruits have the same number of votes? _____

5. How many students voted in total?

_____

6. Use the data from the table to complete the block graph.

Favourite Colour	Number of Students
Red	20 less than blue
Blue	70
Green	50
Yellow	10 less than green

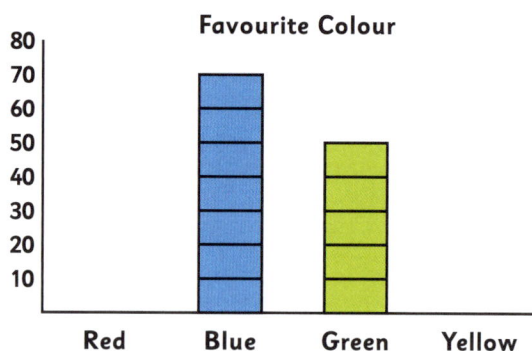

Favourite Colour

7. Which colour is the least popular?

_____

8. How many students like green and yellow combined? _____

9. How many more students like blue than red? _____

10. If 20 more students choose red, which 2 colours will have the same number of votes?

_____ and _____

Wednesday

1. Use the data from the table to complete the bar chart.

Favourite Sport	Number of Students
Football	80
Basketball	20 less than football
Swimming	50
Tennis	Same as swimming

Favourite Sport

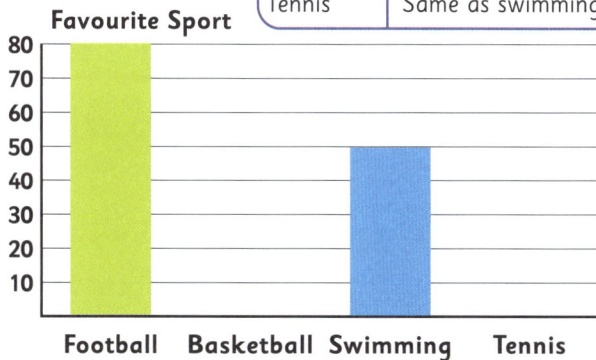

2. _____ is the most popular.

3. How many more students like football than tennis? _____

4. Which 2 sports have an equal number of votes? _____ _____

5. _____ students voted in total.

6. Complete the block chart to show that 40 less students like English than Maths.

Favourite Subject

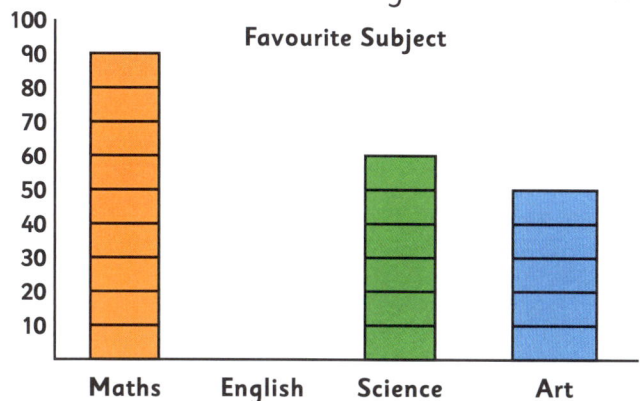

7. _____ is the least popular.

8. How many students like Science and Art combined? ____

9. ____ more students like Maths than English.

10. If 30 more students choose Science, it will have equal votes with _____.

Thursday

Favourite Pets

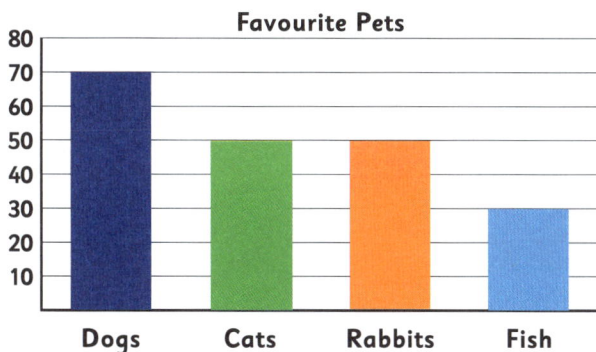

1. Which pet is the least popular? _____

2. Which pet is the most popular? _____

3. How many more students like dogs than rabbits? _____

4. Which 2 pets have equal votes? _____ _____

5. How many students voted in total? _____

Favourite Drinks

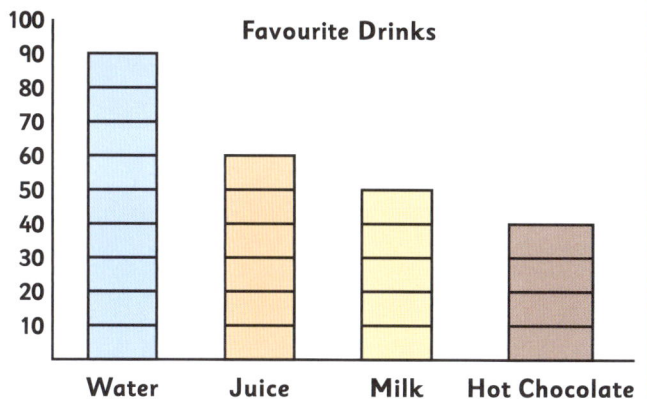

6. _____ is the most popular drink.

7. _____ is the least popular drink.

8. How many students like juice and milk combined? ____

9. How many more students like water than hot chocolate? ____

10. If 30 more students choose juice, which 2 drinks will have equal votes? _____ _____

Monday | Look Back

1. A bakery sold 672 loaves of bread on Monday and 395 loaves on Tuesday. How many loaves of bread did it sell altogether? _____

2. There are 850 students in a school. 476 students go on a field trip. How many students are left at school? _____

3. How many Mondays are there in October? ___

4. How many days are in October? ____

October

M	T	W	T	F	S	S
		1	2	3	4	5
6	7	8	9	10	11	12
13	14	15	16	17	18	19
20	21	22	23	24	25	26
27	28	29	30	31		

5. How many Wednesdays are in October? ___

6. $4.7 + 3.5 =$ _____

7. $8.6 - 2.3 =$ _____

8. A library has 976 books. 587 books are checked out. How many books are left in the library? _____

9. A farmer has 562 potatoes in her basket. She digs 438 more potatoes. How many potatoes does she have in total? _____

10. $5.9 + 2.8 =$ _____

Tuesday

1. Draw a horizontal line that is 4 cm long.

2. Draw a vertical line that is 3 cm long.

3. Draw a diagonal line that is 5 cm long.

4. Draw 2 parallel lines that are 2 cm apart.

5. Draw two perpendicular lines that meet at a right angle.

6. Mark all the acute angles on this triangle.

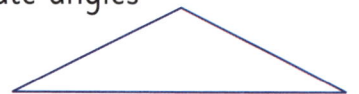

7. Mark with an **X** any obtuse angles on the triangle in question 6.

8. How many right angles does the triangle in question 6 have? _____

9. Ring the smallest angle.

   right   acute   obtuse

10. Sketch one example of parallel lines and one example of perpendicular lines.

Wednesday

1. How many straight sides does a hexagon have? ___

2. How many curved sides does a circle have? ___

3. (a) How many angles does a square have? ___

   (b) Are they right, acute or obtuse angles? _____

4. Draw a rectangle and mark all the right angles.

5. What is the difference between a rhombus and a rectangle? _____ _____

6. Which shape has only one curved edge and one straight edge? _____

7. Does an oval have straight or curved sides? _____

8. What do you call a shape with six straight sides? _____

9. A rhombus has 4 equal sides and opposite angles are the same.
   True ☐   False ☐

10. (a) Draw a polygon with six sides.

    (b) What is a six-sided polygon called? _____

Thursday

1. How many straight sides does a rhombus have? _____

2. Does a square always have 4 right angles?
   Yes ☐   No ☐

3. A regular hexagon has 6 angles. Are they right, acute or obtuse? _____

4. Draw a triangle with 3 acute angles.

5. How does a hexagon differ from a rectangle? _____ _____

6. Which shape has no straight sides and no corners? _____

7. Draw a semicircle and label its curved and straight edges.

8. Which has more sides?
   Rectangle ☐   Hexagon ☐

9. How many right angles does a rectangle have? _____

10. Ring the 2 shapes with no right angles.

Monday — Look Back

1. $6 \times 2 =$ _____
2. $7 \times 4 =$ _____
3. $9 \times 8 =$ _____
4. $16 \div 2 =$ _____
5. $32 \div 4 =$ _____
6. $64 \div 8 =$ _____

7. Laura has 8 boxes of bubble wands. Each box contains 4 tubes. How many wands does she have in total? _____

8. Sarah has 32 stickers. She shares them equally between 4 friends. How many stickers does each friend get? ___

9. Mary buys 4 boxes of cupcakes. Each box contains 8 cupcakes. She gives half of the cupcakes to her friends. How many cupcakes does she have left? _____

10. Jack's grip tape is 2.5 metres long. Sam's is 3.4 metres long. How much grip tape do they have altogether?

_____

Tuesday

1. What time is shown on the clock? Write it in words and in digital format.

_____

_____ : _____

2. What time is shown on the clock? Write it in words and in digital format.

_____

_____ : _____

3. What time is shown on the clock? Write it in words and in digital format.

_____

_____ : _____

4. What time is shown on the clock? Write it in words and in digital format.

_____

_____ : _____

5. How many minutes are in 2 hours and 15 minutes? _____

6. Mia's favourite TV show begins at quarter past 6. She watches for 15 minutes. At what time does it end?

_____

7. Convert 125 minutes to hours and minutes.

_____ hours _____ minutes

8. A train leaves the station at quarter to 5. It takes 1 hour to get to the next station. At what time does it arrive at the next station?

_____

9. Write the digital times.

(a) Quarter past 9

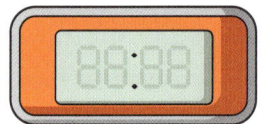

(b) Half past 7

(c) Quarter to 4

10. Match the times.

quarter past 9

half past 3

4 o'clock

quarter to 7

Wednesday

1. Convert 2:00 p.m. to 24-hour time.
   _____

2. Convert 7:45 a.m. to 24-hour time.
   _____

3. Convert 11:30 p.m. to 24-hour time.
   _____

4. Convert 12:15 p.m. to 24-hour time.
   _____

5. Convert 9:20 a.m. to 24-hour time.
   _____

6. A train departs at 4:50 p.m. Write this time in 24-hour format.
   _____

7. A film starts at 10:30 p.m. Write this time in 24-hour format. _____

8. Convert these times to 24-hour format.
   6:10 a.m. _____
   1:45 p.m. _____
   12:00 a.m. (midnight) _____

9. A plane leaves at 5:25 p.m. and the flight lasts 3 hours. At what time will the plane land? Give the answer in 24-hour format. _____

10. Match the 12-hour and 24-hour times.

    | 8:00 a.m. | 15:30 |
    | 12:00 p.m. | 23:15 |
    | 3:30 p.m. | 08:00 |
    | 11:15 p.m. | 12:00 |

Thursday

1. Show 14:05 on the clock. What is the time in words?
   _____

2. Show 04:10 on the clock. What is the time in words?
   _____

3. The clock shows quarter past 9 (a.m.). Write this time in digital format.

4. The clock shows half past 3 (p.m.). Write this time in digital format.

5. If the time is 06:25, what time will it be 5 minutes later?

6. If the time is 11:55, what time was it 5 minutes ago?

7. Write the time 5 minutes after quarter past 8 a.m.

8. Match the times in words with their digital format.

five past 7 p.m.	14:50
ten to 3 p.m.	19:05
twenty past 6 a.m.	04:45
quarter to 5 a.m.	06:20

9. The school bell rings at 09:35. How many minutes until 09:50? _____

10. A cartoon starts at 15:20 and lasts for 10 minutes. At what time does it end? Draw your answer on the clock.

Monday | Look Back

1. 5 × 2 = ____

2. 8 × 4 = ____

3. 7 × 8 = ____

4. 18 ÷ 2 = ____

5. 36 ÷ 4 = ____

6. 48 ÷ 8 = ____

7. A baker makes 9 trays of scones. Each tray holds 4 scones. How many scones are there in total? ____

8. Liam has 40 books. He puts them into 4 equal groups. How many books are in each group? ____

9. Clodagh buys 3 packs of stickers. Each pack contains 8 stickers. She gives 12 stickers to her friend. How many stickers does she have left? ____

10. A wooden plank is 3.6 metres long. Another plank is 2.8 metres long. What is the total length of both planks together? _____

Tuesday

January

Monday	Tuesday	Wednesday	Thursday	Friday	Saturday	Sunday
1	2	3	4	5	6	7
8	9	10	11	12	13	14
15	16	17	18	19	20	21
22	23	24	25	26	27	28
29	30	31				

July

Monday	Tuesday	Wednesday	Thursday	Friday	Saturday	Sunday
1	2	3	4	5	6	7
8	9	10	11	12	13	14
15	16	17	18	19	20	21
22	23	24	25	26	27	28
29	30	31				

1. (a) How many Sundays are there in January? ___

   (b) How many Tuesdays are there in January? ___

2. (a) What day of the week is 15th January? _____

   (b) What day of the week is 4th January? ___

3. How many days are there from 10th January to 20th January? ____

4. (a) What is the date 8 days after 5th January? _____

   (b) What is the date one week before 24th January? _____

   (c) What is the date 5 days before the last Monday in January?

   _____

5. How many Saturdays are there in July?

   ___

6. What day of the week is 21st July?

   _____

7. How many days are there between 2nd July and 15th July? ___

8. What day of the week is 31st July?

   _____

9. Julieta is going away on Friday 10th April and will return on Monday 13th April. How many days will she be away? ___

10. A local library is closed for building work from 1st June to 7th June. They will reopen on 8th June. How many days is the library closed? ___

Wednesday

Train Number	From	To	Departure Time	Arrival Time
101	Station A	Station B	8:00 a.m.	9:30 a.m.
102	Station A	Station C	10:00 a.m.	11:45 a.m.
103	Station B	Station A	12:15 p.m.	1:50 p.m.
104	Station C	Station A	2:30 p.m.	4:00 p.m.
105	Station B	Station C	4:45 p.m.	6:00 p.m.

1. What time does Train 101 leave from Station A? _____

2. Which train arrives at Station B at 9:30 a.m.? _____

3. How long does Train 102 take to travel from Station A to Station C? _____ hrs _____ mins

4. What is the arrival time for Train 103 at Station A? _____

5. Which train departs from Station B at 12:15 p.m.? _____

6. How many trains travel from Station A to Station B? _____

7. What time does Train 104 depart from Station C? _____

8. Which train arrives at Station C at 6:00 p.m.? _____

9. How long does Train 105 take to travel from Station B to Station C? _____ hrs _____ mins

10. What time does Train 103 leave from Station B? _____

Thursday

Monday Timetable	
08:40	School starts
08:40–08:50	SPHE
08:50–09:20	English
09:20–09:55	Gaeilge
09:55–10:10	Story time and Snack
10:10–10:30	Yard 1
10:30–11:00	Maths
11:00–11:30	P.E.
11:30–11:55	Music
11:55–12:10	Story time and Lunch
12:10–12:30	Yard 2
12:30–13:00	Geography
13:00–13:30	Science
13:30–14:20	Art
14:20	Home time

1. What time does the school day start? _____

2. How long does English class last? _____

3. What subject comes after Geography? _____

4. What time is snack break? _____

5. How long is the morning yard break? _____ mins

6. What subject is taught before lunch? _____

7. What time is lunch? _____

8. How many yard breaks are there during the day? _____

9. When is the last class of the day? _____

10. What time does the school day end (home time)? _____

Monday | Look Back

1. 427 + 289 = _____

2. 653 − 378 = _____

3. Lola buys a book for €2.45 and a pencil for €0.80. How much does she spend in total? _____

4. Shane has €2. He buys a drink for €1.25. How much change does he get?

   _____

5. 4.7 + 2.3 = _____

6. Which decimal is greater: 0.9 or 0.4?

   _____

7. Convert 3:45 p.m. to 24-hour format.

   _____

8. What is 14:30 in 12-hour format?

   _____

9. It is 10:25. How many minutes until 11:00? _____

10. The school bell rings at quarter past 2. What time is that in digital format?

Tuesday

1. 4 × 5 = _____

2. 3 × 5 = _____

3. There are 6 rails of t-shirts in a shop. Each rail has 5 t-shirts. How many t-shirts are there altogether? _____

4. A toy store sells toy cars in packs of 5. If Cara buys 7 packs, how many toy cars does she have? _____

5. Ms Kennedy's classroom has 8 tables. There are 5 chairs around each table. How many chairs are there in total?

   _____

6. Riverside tennis club has 9 tennis courts. At a summer camp, there were 5 players on each court. How many players were there altogether?

   _____

7. Five trains arrive into Heuston station every hour. How many trains arrive in 10 hours? _____

8. 7 × 10 = _____

9. A shop sells pencils in packs of 10. If Kate buys 6 packs of pencils, how many pencils will she have? _____

10. Ben's school has 9 bike racks. Each rack can fit 10 bikes. How many bikes can fit into all the bike racks? _____

Wednesday

1. 3 × 3 = _____

2. 5 × 3 = _____

3. A bakery makes 3 loaves of bread each hour. How many loaves are made in 6 hours? ____

4. Elif has 7 boxes. In each box she has 3 medals. How many medals does she have in total? ____

5. 7 × 6 = ____

6. 9 × 6 = ____

7. Mary wants to arrange 3 flowers per vase. She has 8 vases. How many flowers does she need?
____

8. A farm has 6 chicken coops. There are 5 chickens in each coop. How many chickens are there altogether? ____

9. You get 6 glasses of juice from one bottle. How many glasses of juice can you get from 8 bottles? ____

10. A fruit seller sells oranges in bags of 6. If she sells 12 bags, how many oranges does she sell in total? ____

Thursday

1. Draw an array to show 2 × 7.

2. 5 × 7 = ____

3. A farmer has 6 rows of carrots. Each row has 7 carrots. How many carrots does he have in total? ____

4. How many days are there in 8 weeks?
____

5. A bakery sells 7 sausage rolls every hour for 7 hours. How many sausage rolls do they sell? ____

6. A factory packs 9 toys in each box. If they pack 12 boxes, how many toys are packed in total? ____

7. Draw an array to show 4 × 9.

8. 6 × 9 = ____

9. A school has 8 classrooms and each classroom has 9 desks. How many desks are there in total?

   (a) Write a repeated addition sentence for this problem.

   _____

   _____

   (b) Write a multiplication sentence for this problem. _____

   _____

10. There are 10 shelves in a library. Each shelf holds 9 books. How many books are there in total? ____

Monday — Look Back

1. 5 × 7 = _____

2. 4 × 10 = _____

3. 6 pizzas are each cut into 9 equal slices. How many slices are there in total? _____

4. One carton of orange juice holds $\frac{1}{4}$ l. How much does 3 cartons hold?

☐
☐

5. Ring the longest measurement.

606 cm   6 m   6 m 60 cm   6 m 06 cm

6. How many hours and minutes in 75 minutes?

_____ hours _____ minutes

7. How many minutes in 2 hours and 5 minutes?

_____ minutes

8. A hockey team trains 9 hours per week. How many hours do they train in 3 weeks?

_____

9. A film starts at 2:20 p.m. and lasts 1 hour 20 minutes. At what time does it end? _____

10. (a) A train leaves the station at 10:50 a.m. and arrives at the next station at 1:10 p.m. How long is the journey?

_____

(b) If the train was delayed by 15 minutes, at what time would it arrive?

_____

Tuesday

1. 15 + 12 = 28 − 1

True ☐ False ☐

2. Write the correct symbol: =, < or >.

6 × 3 ☐ 20

3. Write + or −.

25 ☐ 10 = 15

4. Complete the equation.

9 × ☐ = 27

5. 18 ÷ 2 = 9

True ☐   False ☐

6. Write the correct symbol: =, <, or >.

32 ☐ 18 + 15

7. Find the missing value.

14 + ☐ = 30

8. Complete the equation.

40 − ☐ = 22

9. 4 × 5 = 10 + 10

True ☐   False ☐

10. Write the correct symbol: =, < or >.

19 + 6 ☐ 30 − 8

Wednesday

1. 48 − 9 = 39

True ☐   False ☐

2. Write the correct symbol: =, < or >.

70 ☐ 35 × 2

3. Write the correct symbol: × or ÷.

24 ☐ 8 = 3

4. Complete the equation.

50 ÷ ☐ = 10

5. 6 × 8 = 48

True ☐   False ☐

6. Write the correct symbol: =, < or >.

75 − 20 ☐ 54 + 1

7. Find the missing value.

33 + ☐ = 60

8. Complete the equation.

72 ÷ ☐ = 9

9. 10 × 5 = 60 − 10

True ☐   False ☐

10. Write the correct symbol: =, <, or >.

58 − 19 ☐ 25 + 12

Thursday

1. 82 − 34 = 48

True ☐   False ☐

2. Write the correct symbol: =, <, or >.

90 ☐ 10 × 8

3. Write the missing symbol (+ or −).

77 ☐ 33 = 44

4. Complete the equation.

99 ÷ ☐ = 11

5. 12 × 7 = 84

True ☐   False ☐

6. Write the correct symbol: =, < or >.

95 − 25 ☐ 40 + 30

7. Find the missing value.

66 + ☐ = 92

8. Complete the equation.

100 − ☐ = 73

9. 8 × 9 = 80 − 8

True ☐   False ☐

10. Write the correct symbol: =, < or >.

50 + 24 ☐ 90 − 15

Monday | Look Back

1. 428 + 275 = _____

2. 732 − 468 = _____

3. A survey shows that 15 students like football, 9 like basketball and 12 like swimming. How many students were surveyed in total? _____

4. An alarm clock shows 7:45 a.m. What time will it be in 25 minutes?

   _____

5. 1 hour 35 minutes + 5 hours 5 minutes = _____ hours _____ minutes

6. A pencil is 4.2 cm long and a crayon is 5.8 cm long. What is their total length end-to-end? _____

7. Draw a vertical line that is no greater than 6 cm. Write its length.

8. 5.7 + 3.4 = _____

9. 8.9 − 2.6 = _____

10. A bus leaves at 3:15 p.m. and arrives at 5:45 p.m. How long is the journey?

   _____

Tuesday

1. How much altogether? €_____

2. How much altogether? €_____

3. How much altogether? €_____

4. Maeve buys a toy for €3.20. She pays with a €5 note. How much change does she get? _____

5. Liam buys a sandwich for €2.80 and a drink for €1.50. How much does he spend in total? _____

6. A book costs €5.00. Ella has €1.80. How much more money does Ella need to be able to buy the book?

   _____

7. Ben has €3.60. He finds 40c on the ground. How much does he have now? €_____

8. Sarah buys a chocolate bar for €1.95. How much change does she get from €5? €_____

9. David buys stickers for €2.10 and a notebook for €1.75. How much does he spend in total? €_____

10. A pack of markers costs €4.20. How much change would you get from €5?

   _____

Wednesday

1. How much in total? €_____

2. How much in total? €_____

3. How much in total? €_____

4. Alex buys a book for €6.50 and a pen for €2.40. How much does he spend? €_____

5. A toy costs €7.80. How much change would you get from €10? €_____

6. Katie has €9.25 and spends €4.60. How much money does she have left? €_____

7. Max buys a meal for €5.90 and a drink for €2.20. How much does he spend in total? €_____

8. How much in total? €_____

9. How much in total? €_____

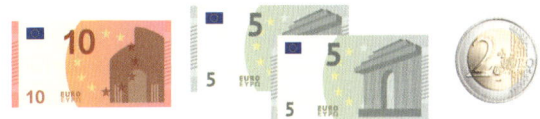

10. How much in total? €_____

Thursday

1. How much in total? €_____

2. How much in total? €_____

3. You have one €50 note, and you spend €20. How much do you have now? €_____

4. Farah is saving for a new bike that costs €48. She already has €35. How much more does she need? €_____

5. A family buys 3 cinema tickets for €15 each. How much do they pay altogether? €_____

6. A toy shop sells a skateboard for €28.50 and a helmet for €14.25. What is the total cost? €_____

7. Matei has €50. He spends €23.80 on clothes and €12.40 on lunch. How much money does he have left? €_____

8. A bakery sells cakes for €18.60, pastries for €9.90 and a loaf of bread for €4.50. What is the total if you buy a cake, a pastry and a loaf? €_____

9. Which 2 items can you buy for less than €50?

_____

_____

€38
€50
€11

10. Emily has a €50 note. She buys a jacket for €28.00. How much change does she get? €_____

Monday | Look Back

1. What is the value of 7 in the number 749? _____

2. Write the number six hundred and forty-two in digits. _____

3. What number is 300 more than 384? _____

4. If a clock shows 3:45, what time will it be in 15 minutes?

   _____

5. School starts at 9:00 a.m. and ends at 2:30 p.m. How many hours and minutes is the school day?

   _____

6. How many sides does a hexagon have? __

7. Which 2-D shape has 4 equal sides and 4 right angles? _____

8. Amy ate $\frac{1}{4}$ of a pizza. How much of the pizza is left? ☐☐

9. Jack shared 8 apples equally between himself and 3 friends.
   What fraction of the apples does each person get? ☐☐

10. A cake is cut into 8 equal pieces. Tom eats 3 pieces. What fraction of the cake did he eat? ☐☐

Tuesday

1. Record the total. _____

2. Record the total. _____

3. Record the total. _____

4. Record the total. _____

5. Record the total. _____

6. Lauren buys a toy for €30.50 and a book for €12.40. How much does she spend in total? €_____

7. John has €48.20. He earns €24.30 doing some chores. How much money does John have now? €_____

8. Emmet buys a pencil case for €11.90 and a ruler for €15.60. How much does he pay in total? €_____

9. Lia has €56.50. She buys a jacket for €32.40. How much money does she have left? €_____

10. Lucy buys the same jacket as Lia in the sale. The original price has been reduced by $\frac{1}{2}$. How much does Lucy pay for the jacket? €_____

Wednesday

1. Record the total. _____

2. Record the total. _____

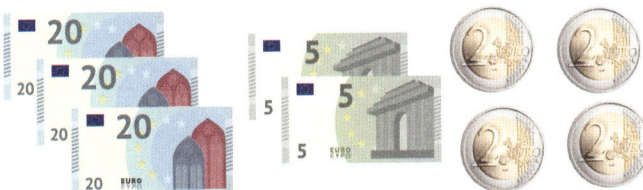

3. Record the total. _____

4. Record the total. _____

5. Record the total. _____

6. Sam buys a shirt for €32.50. He pays with a €50 note. How much change will he get? _____

7. Nila buys a toy for €18.00. She pays with a €50 note. How much change will she get? _____

8. Jack buys a book for €27.50. He pays with a €50 note. How much change will he get? _____

9. Lisa buys a jacket for €40.00. She pays with a €50 note. How much change will she get? _____

10. Ade buys a pair of shoes for €12.50. He pays with a €50 note. How much change will he get? _____

Thursday

1. How much altogether? _____

2. Tom has three €2 coins and €1.50 in other coins. How much money does he have in total? _____

3. A 4-pack of highlighters costs €10. A single highlighter costs €2.80. How much do you save by buying the pack instead of 4 singles? € _____

4. A pack of 6 brushes costs €18. A single brush costs €3.50. Which option is better value? _____

5. 4 notebooks cost €12. What is the unit price? € _____

6. How much altogether? _____

7. Write 2 amounts that total €5.78.
_____ _____

8. Round to the nearest euro:
(a) €9.55 € ____
(b) €2.21 € ____

9. (a) €51.00 + €32.00 = _____
(b) €13.25 + €12.25 = _____
(c) €41.70 + €0.95 = _____

10. Write notes and coins to represent €64.33.
_____
_____

Monday | Look Back

1. Ms Mannion has 7 boxes of pencils. Each box contains 5 pencils. How many pencils are there in total? ____

2. (a) A train has 10 passengers in each carriage. How many passengers are there in 6 carriages? ____

   (b) 2 extra carriages are added. How many passengers can the train carry now? ____

3. One spider has 8 legs. How many legs do 5 spiders have? ____

4. Tick the better value option.

   4 cookies for €8 ☐

   8 cookies for €12 ☐

5. 6 tennis balls cost €12. What is the unit price? €____

6. One week has 7 days. How many days are in 6 weeks? ____

7. Convert 350 cm to metres and centimetres. _____ m _____ cm

8. Convert 4.2 metres to centimetres. _____ cm

9. Compare the numbers using >, < or =.

   6.3 ☐ 6.5

   4.8 ☐ 4.80

10. 2.4 + 3.5 = _____

Tuesday

1. 50 ÷ 5 = ___

2. 30 ÷ 5 = ___

3. 80 ÷ 10 = ____

4. 100 ÷ 10 = ____

5. A pack of 50 pencils is shared equally between 5 students. How many pencils does each student get? ____

6. There are 40 chairs in the assembly hall. The principal asks Hugh to arrange them in rows of 10. How many rows can Hugh make? ___

7. Sophie has 25 erasers and shares them between 5 friends. How many will each friend get? ___

8. A bakery packs 60 buns into boxes of 10. How many boxes are needed? ___

9. A toy shop has 90 toy cars on display, with 10 cars on each shelf. How many shelves are there? ___

10. (a) A farmer has 48 eggs and packs them into cartons of 6. How many cartons does he fill? ___

    (b) How many cartons could he fill if he packed eggs into cartons of 12? ____

Wednesday

1. $18 \div 3 = $ ___

2. $24 \div 3 = $ ___

3. $30 \div 3 = $ ___

4. $36 \div 6 = $ ___

5. $42 \div 6 = $ ___

6. A class of 27 students is divided into groups of 3. How many groups are there? ___

7. Lily makes 36 bracelets and puts them into bags of 6. How many bags does she need? ___

8. Liam has made 54 jars of slime. He packs them in boxes of 6. How many boxes does he use? ___

9. A coach has 36 seats. If 3 people can sit in each row, how many rows are there? ___

10. A teacher has 21 stickers and gives them out in packs of 3. How many students receive a pack? ___

Thursday

1. $49 \div 7 = $ ___

2. $35 \div 7 = $ ___

3. $28 | 7$
   □

4. $81 | 9$
   □

5. $\dfrac{63}{9} = $ ___

6. $\dfrac{56}{8} = $ ___

7. (a) A farmer has 50 strawberries divides them equally into 7 baskets. How many full baskets can she make? ___

(b) How many strawberries are left over? ___

(c) Write a division sentence to record how the strawberries were divided.

_____

_____

8. Matt has 26 cherries and wants to share them equally between 6 friends.

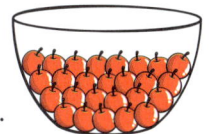

(a) Write a division sentence to match this problem.

_____

_____

(b) How many cherries does each friend get? ___

(c) How many are left over? ___

9. A coach has 31 people on board. Each row has 4 seats.

(a) How many rows are full? ___

(b) How many rows are not full? ___

10. A board game has 22 counters. Barry arranges them in stacks of 5.

(a) How many stacks of 5 counters are there? ___

(b) How many counters are left over? ___

Monday Look Back

1. Milana buys a monitor for €236 and a games console for €487. How much does she spend altogether? _____

2. A farmer has 865 sheep. He sells 429 at the market. How many sheep does he have left? _____

3. A school library has 324 fiction books and 298 non-fiction books. How many books are there in total? _____

4. Jake's football team scored 739 points last year. This year, they scored 584 points. How many fewer points did they score this year than last year?

   _____

5. $21 \div 4 =$ ___ (R___)

6. $50 \div 8 =$ ___ (R___)

7. $\frac{56}{8} =$ _____

8. Write a 3-digit number that has 3 in the units place. _____

9. What time in the morning does the clock show?

   _____

10. Show twenty-five past three on the analogue clock.

Tuesday

1. Write 'certain,' 'likely,' 'even chance,' 'unlikely,' or 'impossible' for each event.
   (a) The sun will rise tomorrow.

   _____

   (b) You will grow wings and fly.

   _____

   (c) It will rain in the next year.

   _____

2. Tick which is more likely to happen.
   Rolling a 6 ☐
   Rolling an even number ☐

3. Tick the event that has an even chance of happening.
   Flipping a coin and landing on heads. ☐
   Rolling a 6 on a dice. ☐

4. You have a bag of 9 red, 5 blue and 1 yellow sweets. If you pick one sweet at random, which colour are you most likely to get? _____

5. In a box of 10 pencils, 5 are green, 2 are red and 3 are blue. Which colour is least likely to be picked?

   _____

6. A spinner has 4 red sections, 3 blue sections and 1 yellow section. Which colour is it most likely to land on?

   _____

7. Tick the event that is impossible.

   Rolling a number greater than 6 on a 6-sided dice. ☐

   Rolling a number less than 7 on a 6-sided dice. ☐

8. If you throw a ball in the air, it will fall back down? Ring the correct answer.

   Certain   Likely   Unlikely

9. A bag has only blue marbles. Ring the chance of picking a red marble.

   Likely   Unlikely   Impossible

10. The weather forecast says there is a 50% chance of rain tomorrow. Is it certain, likely, even chance, unlikely or impossible that it will rain?

   _____

Wednesday

1. Write 'certain,' 'likely,' 'even chance,' 'unlikely,' or 'impossible' for each event.

   (a) A cat will bark. _____

   (b) You will eat lunch today.
   _____

   (c) Our class will have homework.
   _____

   (d) It will snow in the summer.
   _____

2. Tick the more likely event.
   Rolling a number > 2 ☐
   Rolling a 1 ☐

3. When flipping a coin, what is the probability it will land on tails?
   _____

4. A bag contains 6 pink, 2 blue and 2 green marbles. What is the chance of picking a blue marble?
   _____

Look at the spinner and answer the questions.

5. What is the chance of landing on pink?
   _____

6. Which colour is the spinner least likely to land on? _____

7. Which colour is the spinner most likely to land on? _____

8. Ring the chance of landing on purple.

   certain   likely   unlikely   impossible

9. Ring the chance of landing on yellow.

   certain   likely   unlikely   impossible

10. Colour the spinner so that there is an even chance of landing on each colour.

Thursday

1. Write 'certain,' 'likely,' 'even chance,' 'unlikely,' or 'impossible' for each event.
   (a) Tomorrow it will rain.
   _____

   (b) A dice will land on 7.
   _____

   (c) A dog will wag its tail.
   _____

2. A spinner has 5 equal sections: 2 red, 1 blue and 2 green. What colour are you most likely to land on?
   _____

3. A bag has 4 blue, 4 green and 4 red marbles. What is the chance of picking a green marble? _____

4. In a bag of 10 sweets, 9 are strawberry and 1 is lemon. What flavour are you most likely to pick?
   _____

5. When rolling a regular dice, what is the chance of landing on an odd number?
   _____

6. A deck of 52 cards has 4 suits: ♥♠♦♣. What are the chances of choosing a heart? _____

7. A jar contains 20 counters: 10 blue, 7 red, 2 green and 1 yellow. Which colour is least likely to be picked?
   _____

8. Tick the event has an even chance.
   Winter will follow autumn. ☐
   You will win the lottery. ☐

9. Tick the event that is certain.
   The sun will set today. ☐
   You will have pizza for dinner. ☐

10. Write something that is impossible.
    _____

Monday Look Back

1. What time in the morning is shown on this clock?

   (a) Write your answer in words.

   _____

   (b) Write this your answer in digital format.

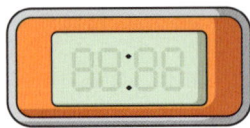

2. Ben goes to football training at 3:30 p.m. What time is that in 24-hour format? _____

3. Draw clock hands to show 07:15.

4. Ring the correct answer. A right angle is:

   Less than 90°   More than 90°   90°

5. Name a shape that has 4 equal sides and 4 right angles. _____

6. A hexagon has ___ sides and ___ vertices.

7. 6 × 4 = ____

8. If 20 apples are shared equally between 5 friends, how many apples will each friend get? ____

9. ___ ÷ 3 = 7

10. Which fraction has the greater value: $\frac{1}{2}$ or $\frac{3}{4}$? Explain. _____

    _____

Tuesday

1. This is a _____ line.

2. This is a _____ line.

3. This is a pair of _____ lines.

4. This is a pair of _____ lines.

5. This is a _____ angle.

6. This is an _____ angle.

7. This is an _____ angle.

8. Draw a pair of parallel lines.

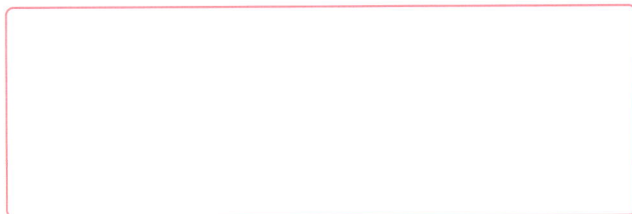

9. Draw a pair of perpendicular lines.

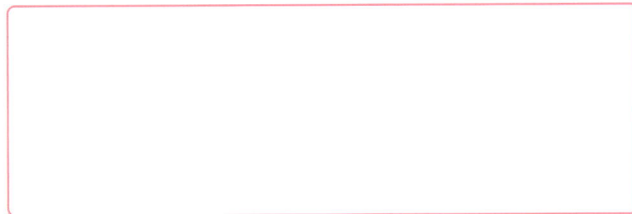

10. (a) Mark all angles with an X.
    (b) How many are right angles? ___
    (c) How many are acute angles? ___
    (d) How many obtuse angles? ___

Wednesday

1. Tick the turn shown.
$\frac{1}{4}$ turn clockwise ☐
$\frac{1}{2}$ turn clockwise ☐
Full turn clockwise ☐

2. Tick the turn shown.
$\frac{1}{2}$ turn clockwise ☐
$\frac{3}{4}$ turn anticlockwise ☐
Full turn clockwise ☐

3. Tick the turn shown.
$\frac{1}{4}$ turn clockwise ☐
$\frac{3}{4}$ turn clockwise ☐
$\frac{1}{2}$ turn clockwise ☐

4. Tick the turn shown.
Full turn clockwise ☐
$\frac{3}{4}$ turn clockwise ☐
$\frac{1}{2}$ turn clockwise ☐

5. Tick the turn shown.
$\frac{1}{4}$ turn anticlockwise ☐
$\frac{1}{4}$ turn clockwise ☐

6. Tick the turn shown. ☐
$\frac{1}{4}$ turn anticlockwise ☐
$\frac{3}{4}$ turn clockwise ☐
Full turn anticlockwise ☐

7. Tick the turn shown.
$\frac{1}{2}$ turn clockwise ☐
$\frac{1}{2}$ turn anticlockwise ☐

8. Tick the turn shown.
$\frac{3}{4}$ turn anticlockwise ☐
$\frac{1}{4}$ turn anticlockwise ☐
Full turn clockwise ☐

9. Tick the turn shown.
$\frac{1}{4}$ turn clockwise ☐
$\frac{1}{4}$ turn anticlockwise ☐

10. A full turn brings you back to the start.
True ☐ False ☐

Thursday

1. Name a county north of Limerick.
_____

2. Name a county south of Limerick.
_____

3. Name a county east of Limerick.
_____

4. Name a county west of Limerick.
_____

5. Write the missing compass points.

6. What direction is the opposite of North (N)? _____

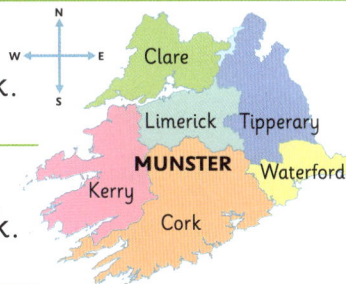

7. Ring all the directions that have 'west' in them:

Southeast   Southwest   North   Northwest   East

8. Draw an arrow pointing East (E) from the centre of this box.

9. Which direction is between North and East? _____

10. Write the opposite of each direction.

Direction	Opposite
Southeast	
East	
Northwest	

Monday | Look Back

1. 6 × 9 = ____

2. 72 ÷ 8 = ____

3. One notebook costs €3. How much would 7 notebooks cost? ____

4. Sally has €20. She buys a book for €7.25.

   (a) How much money does she have left? €_____

   (b) Write her change in notes and coins.

   _____

   _____

   _____

   _____

5. Write the correct symbol: <, = or >.

   €18.75 ☐ €18.57

6. Liam buys 4 chocolate bars at 75c each. What is the total cost? _____

7. What time is shown on the clock? Write your answer in words.

   _____

   _____

8. Mark's piano lesson starts at 3:15 p.m. and lasts 50 minutes. At what time does it end? _____

9. (a) Mia earns €8 a week babysitting. How much will she earn in 6 weeks? _____

   (b) Mia's older sister earns €12 a week babysitting. How much will she earn in 6 weeks? _____

10. Cian receives €20 pocket money per month and saved all of it for 4 months. How much did he save? _____

Tuesday

5 | | 🚲 | | | |
4 | 🏪 | | | 🐱 | |
3 | | | 🌳 | | |
2 | | 🐕 | | | |
1 | 🏠 | | 🪑 | | ⚽ |
 | A | B | C | D | E |

1. Which object is at C1? _____

2. Which object is at E1? _____

3. Which object is at A4? _____

4. Which object is at B2? _____

5. Which object is at D4? _____

6. Write the grid reference for the house.

   _____

7. Write the grid reference for the bicycle.

   _____

8. Which object is closest to the bike?

   _____

9. Which 2 objects have grid references beginning with C? _____ and

   _____

10. Draw a sun at E5.

Wednesday

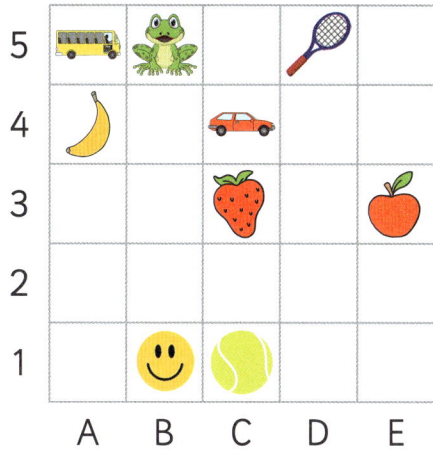

1. Which symbol is at B1? _____

2. Which square has the 🐸? _____

3. Which object is at E3? _____

4. Where is the 🍌 ? Write the grid reference. _____

5. Which object is at C4? _____

6. Write the grid reference for the 🚌. _____

7. Draw a sad face at E2. _____

8. Write the grid reference for the 🍓. ____

9. Which object is at D5? _____

10. Which object is at C1. _____

Thursday

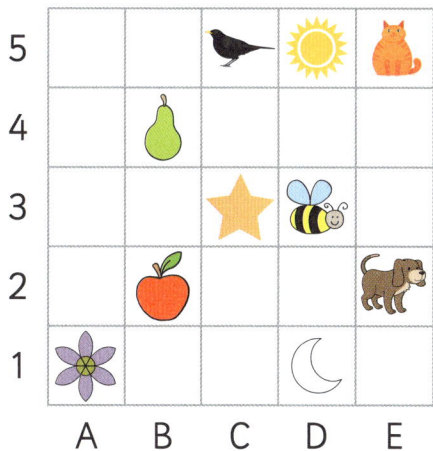

1. Which object is at A1? _____

2. Write the grid reference for the ☀. _____

3. Write the grid reference for the 🌙. _____

4. Which object is at D3? _____

5. Which object is at C5? _____

6. Write the grid reference for the ⭐. _____

7. Which object is at B4? _____

8. Which is at E2? _____

9. Write the grid reference for the 🐝. _____

10. What is located at E5? _____

Monday — Look Back

1. $7 \times 8 =$ _____

2. $90 \div 10 =$ _____

3. A pack of crayons costs €2. How much do 10 packs cost? _____

4. Isobel bought a toy for €3.50. How much change did she get from €10? _____

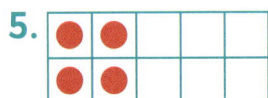

5.
   (a) Write the number of counters in the frame as a fraction. ☐/☐
   (b) Write the number of counters as a decimal fraction. _____
6. Write six hundred and four in digits. _____

7. Draw an even number on the abacus that has 7 in the tens place.

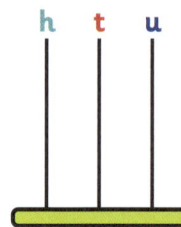

   h t u

8. Charlie's music lesson starts at 4:00 p.m. and lasts 1 hour 20 minutes. At what time does it finish? _____

9. Fill in the missing numbers.
   (a) 20, 40, 60, ____, ____, 120
   (b) 105, 107, ____, ____, 113, 115
   (c) 555, 550, 545, 540, ____, ____

10. Billy earns €10 a week dog-walking. How much will he earn in 4 weeks? _____

Tuesday

1. How many $\frac{1}{4}$ kg equal 1 kg? _____

2. Ring the heavier weight.

   $\frac{1}{2}$ kg $\frac{1}{4}$ kg?

3. If one watermelon weighs 1 kg, how much would one and a half watermelons weigh? _____ kg

4. Mia's meringue recipe needs 1 kg of sugar. How many $\frac{1}{2}$ kg bags of sugar does she need? _____

5. Mary has 1 kg of apples. She eats $\frac{1}{2}$ kg. How much is left? _____ kg

6. Tom buys 4 punnets of strawberries. Each punnet weighs $\frac{1}{4}$ kg. How much do the 4 punnets weigh? _____ kg

7. Ring the lightest weight.

   1 kg sugar $\frac{1}{2}$ kg salt $\frac{1}{4}$ kg butter

8. How much more is 1 kg than $\frac{1}{2}$ kg? $\frac{\Box}{\Box}$ kg

9. Ben has 2 packets of $\frac{1}{4}$ kg cheese. How much cheese does he have? $\frac{\Box}{\Box}$ kg

10. (a) $\frac{1}{4}$ kg + $\frac{1}{4}$ kg = $\frac{\Box}{\Box}$ kg

    (b) $\frac{1}{2}$ kg + $\frac{1}{2}$ kg = $\frac{\Box}{\Box}$ kg

    (c) 1 kg − $\frac{1}{2}$ kg = $\frac{\Box}{\Box}$ kg

Wednesday

1. 1,000 g = 1 kg
   True ☐   False ☐

2. Ring the heavier weight.
   600 g   450 g

3. Write the correct symbol: <, > or =.
   800 g ☐ 1 kg

4. Nancy's pencil case weighs 750 g. Róisín's pencil case weighs 500 g. Whose pencil case is heavier?
   _____

5. Ring the correct answer.
   1,000 g is the same as:
   10 g   100 g   1 kg

6. Tomás has a box of cereal that weighs 300 g. He buys another that weighs 400 g. What is the total weight of both boxes? _____ g

7. Write the correct symbol: <, > or =.
   250 g ☐ $\frac{1}{4}$ kg

8. Aarav's lunch weighs 1,000 g. Milana's lunch weighs 950 g.
   (a) Whose lunch is heavier?
   _____
   (b) By how much? _____

9. Tadhg's bag holds 2 schoolbooks that weigh 250 g and 500 g. What is the total weight of the books in his bag? _____ g

10. Tick the items that weigh more than 500 g:
    ☐ 200 g apple
    ☐ 700 g bag of flour
    ☐ 1 kg potatoes
    ☐ 300 g packet of biscuits.

Thursday

1.
kg	g
2	250
+ 3	103

2.
kg	g
1	400
+ 2	300

3.
kg	g
4	500
+ 1	200

4.
kg	g
5	610
− 2	305

5.
kg	g
3	425
− 1	110

6.
kg	g
6	700
− 2	500

7.
kg	g
2	825
+ 3	336

8.
kg	g
5	645
− 2	555

9. Billy carried a bag of potatoes weighing 3 kg 750 g. Zach carried a bag weighing 4 kg 350 g. What is the total weight carried by both boys?
   _____

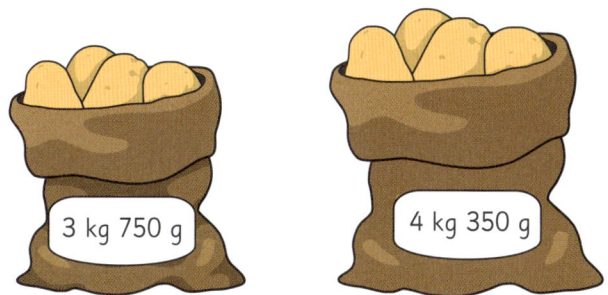

3 kg 750 g   4 kg 350 g

10. Isobel bought a bag of vegetables weighing 5 kg 850 g. She used 2 kg 565 g for dinner. How much does she have left? _____

Monday — Look Back

1. 325 + 248 = _____

2. 603 − 278 = _____

3. The school library has 450 books. 196 are on loan. How many books are left in the library? _____

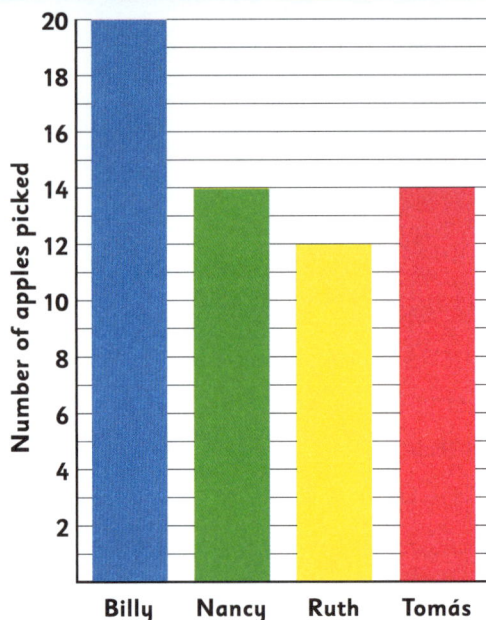

4.
l	ml
8	350
+ 3	125

_____

5.
l	ml
6	204
− 1	101

_____

6. Tadhg has 48 sweets. He shares them equally between 6 friends. How many sweets will each friend get? _____

7. Who picked the most apples?

_____

8. How many more apples did Billy pick than Ruth? _____

9. How many apples did the children pick altogether? _____

10. The children pack all the picked apples into boxes. Each box holds 10 apples. How many boxes do they need? _____

Tuesday

1. 1 litre = _____ ml

2. $\frac{1}{2}$ litre = _____ ml

3. $\frac{1}{4}$ litre = _____ ml

4. $\frac{3}{4}$ litre = _____ ml

5. Write the correct symbol: <, > or =.
   500 ml ☐ $\frac{1}{2}$ l

6. Write the correct symbol: <, > or =.
   250 ml ☐ $\frac{1}{4}$ l

7. How much liquid is in this container?

_____

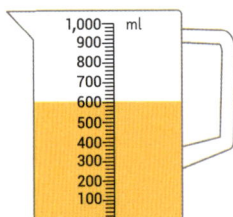

8. How much water is in the jug?
   More than $\frac{1}{2}$ litre ☐
   Less than $\frac{1}{2}$ litre ☐

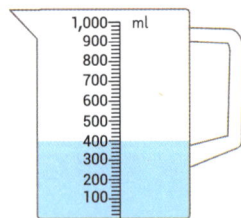

9. Ring the container with the most liquid.

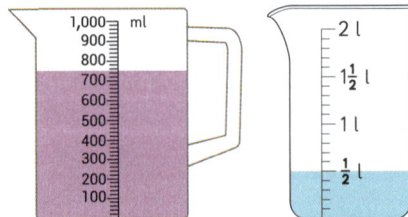

10. Estimate then calculate: If a cup holds 250 ml, how many cups are needed to fill a 1 l jug? _____

Wednesday

1. Write the correct symbol: <, > or =.

   750 ml ☐ 1 l

2. Write the correct symbol: <, > or =.

   500 ml ☐ $\frac{1}{2}$ l

3. Write the correct symbol: <, > or =.

   $\frac{1}{4}$ l ☐ 250 ml

4. Write the correct symbol: <, > or =.

   800 ml ☐ $\frac{3}{4}$ l

5. Mairéad poured 400 ml of water into a jug. She added 100 ml of juice. How much liquid is in the jug altogether?

   _____

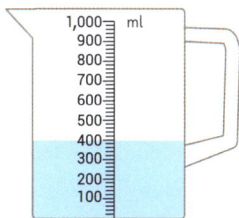

6. Gordon's bottle had 900 ml of water. He drank 300 ml. How much water was left? _____ ml

7. How much water would you need to fill both of these bottles? _____ ml

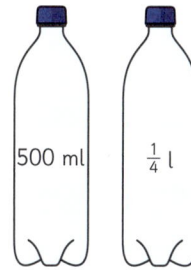

8. Ring the correct answer. $\frac{3}{4}$ l is the same as:

   250 ml   500 ml   750 ml

9. Ring the greatest capacity.

   1 l $\frac{3}{4}$ l $\frac{1}{2}$ l

10. Tilly's watering can has a capacity of 1 litre. She puts 400 ml of plant food into the empy can. How much water does she need to add to fill the can to 1 litre? _____ ml

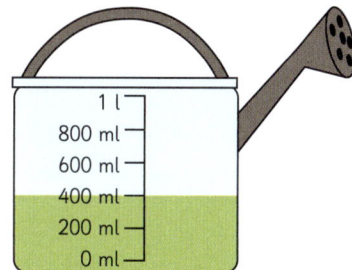

Thursday

1. 1 l 200 ml + 300 ml = ____ l _____ ml
2. 2 l 500 ml + 1 l = ____ l _____ ml
3. 400 ml + 300 ml = ____ l _____ ml
4. 1 l – 500 ml = ____ l _____ ml
5. 2 l – 1 l 200 ml = ____ l _____ ml
6. 3 l – 750 ml = ____ l _____ ml

7.
l	ml
1	855
+ 3	545

   _____

8.
l	ml
3	268
– 1	599

   _____

9. Brendan poured 2 l 300 ml of milk into a carton. He added 1 l 250 ml more. How much milk is in the carton in total? _____

10. Isaac filled a container with 1 l of oil. He used 750 ml for cooking. How much is left? _____ ml

Monday — Look Back

1. What fraction of this shape is coloured:

   (a) purple? _____

   (b) yellow? _____

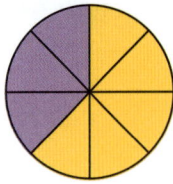

2. How much in total? _____

3. Lisa has €20. She buys an ice cream for herself and each of her 4 friends. How much money does Lisa have left? €_____

   €3

4. Show 03:25 on the analogue clock.

5. Write the correct symbol: <, > or =.

   1 m 25 cm ☐ 115 cm

6. Write the correct symbol: <, > or =.

   755 g ☐ 1 kg 100 g

7. Write the correct symbol: <, > or =.

   1 l ☐ 1,000 ml

8. Write the correct symbol: <, > or =.

   $\frac{2}{5}$ ☐ $\frac{5}{10}$

9. $\frac{1}{3}$ of a number is 6. What's the number? _____

10. Write the missing decimal fractions on the number line.

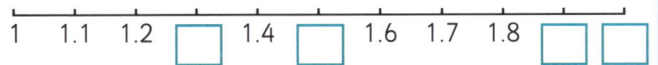

    1   1.1   1.2   ☐   1.4   ☐   1.6   1.7   1.8   ☐   ☐

Tuesday

1. Work out the pattern rule to fill in the blanks.

   12, 16, _____, 24, _____, 32, _____

2. Work out the pattern rule to fill in the blanks.

   45, _____, 65, _____, 85, 95

3. Work out the pattern rule to fill in the blanks.

   _____, 70, _____, 80, _____, 90, _____

4. Complete the pattern by adding the same amount each time.

   _____, 200, _____, _____, 260, 280

5. What is the rule for this pattern?

   100, 220, 340, 460

   _____

6. Continue the pattern using the same subtraction rule.

   90, _____, 70, _____, 50, _____

7. Write the blanks.

   _____, 200, _____, 160, _____, 120

8. Fill in the missing numbers in the subtraction pattern.

   500, _____, _____, 440, 420, _____, 380

9. Complete this subtraction pattern.

   999, _____, _____, 939, 919, _____, 879

10. What is the subtraction rule in this pattern? 600, 550, 500, 450

    _____

Wednesday

1. I am a 2-digit even number less than 70. My digits add up to 11. My first digit is greater than my second digit. ____

2. I am a 2-digit number. My digits add up to 10. My units digit is 4. What number am I? ____

3. I am a 2-digit number less than 90. I am a multiple of 5. My digits add up to 9. My second digit is 5. ____

4. I am a 2-digit number greater than 40 and less than 70. Both my digits are even. They add up to 12. ____

5. I am a 2-digit odd number greater than 30 and less than 90. Both my digits are the same. ____

6. I am a 2-digit number greater than 50. I am a multiple of 3. My digits add up to 12. My first digit is 2 more than my second digit. ____

7. I am a 2-digit odd number greater than 80. My digits add up to 17. My first digit is smaller than my second digit. ____

8. I am a 2-digit number less than 60. My digits add up to 9. My second digit is double my first digit. ____

9. I am a 2-digit number between 60 and 80. Both my digits are odd numbers. Their sum is 12. My second digit is 2 more than the first. ____

10. I am a 2-digit number greater than 40 and less than 70. My digits add up to 11. My second digit is 1 less than my first. ____

Thursday

Make 2 multiplication sentences with each array.

1. ___ × ___ = ____
   ___ × ___ = ____

2. ___ × ___ = ____
   ___ × ___ = ____

3. ___ × ___ = ____
   ___ × ___ = ____

4. ___ × ___ = ____
   ___ × ___ = ____

5. ___ × ___ = ____
   ___ × ___ = ____

Make multiplication and division sentences with the numbers in each triangle.

6. 35 / 7 5
   ____ × ____ = ____
   ____ ÷ ____ = ____

7. 54 / 9 6
   ____ × ____ = ____
   ____ ÷ ____ = ____

8. 48 / 12 4
   ____ × ____ = ____
   ____ ÷ ____ = ____

9. 90 / 10 9
   ____ × ____ = ____
   ____ ÷ ____ = ____

10. 88 / 8 11
    ____ × ____ = ____
    ____ ÷ ____ = ____

Monday | Look Back

1. Lara's bag weighs 5 kg 235 g. Luca's bag is 1 kg 375 g heavier than Lara's. What weight is Luca's bag?
   ___ kg ___ g

2. Simone has 775 ml of water in her bottle. Jack has 525 ml in his bottle. How much water do they have in total? _____ l ___ ml

3. Sara and Ned need 1 m of ribbon. Sara has 35 cm and Ned has 55 cm. How much more ribbon do they need? _____ cm

4. Record 4:30 p.m. using the 24-hour format. _____

5. Aarav had €50. He bought a t-shirt for €12, shorts for €18 and a new pair of socks for €4.50. How much money does he have left? _____

6. I am a 2-D shape. I have 2 short straight sides, 2 long straight sides and 4 vertices. I am a _____.

7. Maeve sells 10 cartons of eggs with 6 eggs in each carton. How many eggs did she sell altogether? _____

8. 81 sweets are shared equally among 9 children. How many sweets did each child get? ____

9. 456 tickets were sold for the first night of the school musical. 307 tickets were sold for the second night. How many tickets were sold in total? _____

10. A library has 788 fiction books and 598 non-fiction books. How many more fiction books are there than non-fiction books? _____

Tuesday

1. This is a _____.

2. This is a _____.

3. This is a _____.

4. This is a _____.

5. This is a _____.

6. This is a _____.

7. This is a _____.

8. This is a _____.

9. (a) Label each vertex.

   (b) How many vertices altogether? ____

10. Look at the shapes in questions 1–8 again. List the ones that roll.

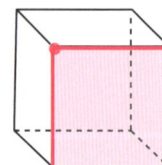

   _____ _____
   _____ _____.

Wednesday

1. I have 1 vertex, 1 circular face and 1 curved surface. I am a _____.

2. I have 2 circular faces, 1 curved surface and no vertices. I am a _____.

3. I have 6 square faces, 12 edges and 8 vertices. All my sides are equal. I am a _____.

4. I have 6 rectangular faces, 12 edges and 8 vertices. My opposite faces are equal. I am a _____.

5. I have no vertices, no edges and 1 curved surface. I am perfectly round. I am a _____.

6. I have 1 square face, 4 triangular faces, 5 vertices and 8 edges. I am a _____.

7. I have 4 triangular faces, 4 vertices and 6 edges. I am a _____.

8. I have 2 triangular faces, 3 rectangular faces, 6 vertices and 9 edges. I am a _____.

9. Write your own set of clues to describe a 3-D object.

_____

_____

10. Draw a real-life 3-D object.

Thursday

1. Which 3-D object does this net make?

_____

2. Which 3-D object does this net make?

_____

3. Which 3-D object does this net make?

_____

4. Which 3-D object does this net make?

_____

5. Which 3-D object does this net make?

_____

6. Which 3-D object does this net make?

_____

7. This is the net of a triangular prism.
True ☐   False ☐

8. Which 2-D shapes make up the net of a triangular prism?

_____ and _____

9. Describe the 2-D shapes that make up the nets of a:
Cylinder: _____
Cone: _____

10. Look at the nets of a rectangular prism and a square-based pyramid. How many faces does each net have?
Retangular prism: _____
Square-based pyramid: _____

Monday | Look Back

1. 56 + 489 = _____
2. 915 − 637 = _____
3. A chart shows that 28 pupils like apples, 34 like bananas and 37 like grapes. How many students were surveyed altogether? _____
4. The school clock shows 2:50 p.m. What time will it be in 40 minutes? _____

5. A train departs at 11:20 a.m. and arrives at 1:55 p.m. How long is the journey? ____ hrs ____ mins

6. What is the value of the underlined digit? 1,651 _____
7. Name this 3-D shape. _____

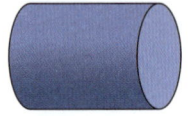

8. $\frac{1}{3}$ of ____ = 10
9. Which 3-D object does this net make? _____

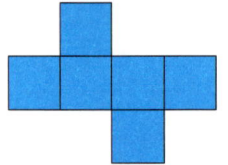

10. Which 3-D object does this net make? _____

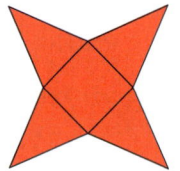

Tuesday

1. An equilateral  has ____ lines of symmetry.

2. A ⬛ has ____ lines of symmetry.

3. A ▭ has ____ lines of symmetry.

4. A ⬡ has ____ lines of symmetry.

5. Ring the asymmetrical image.

6. Draw the line of symmetry on the ribbon.

7. Complete the image to show reflective symmetry.

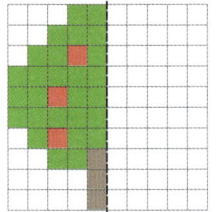

8. Complete the image to show reflective symmetry.

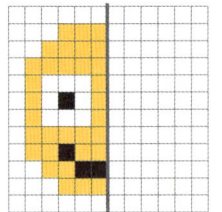

9. Mirror this pattern.

10. Ring the 3 types of transformation.

Translation

Asymmetry

Rotation

Reflection

Wednesday

1. The order of rotational symmetry is ____.

2. The order of rotational symmetry is ____.

3. This letter has been:
   - [ ] Reflected
   - [ ] Rotated
   - [ ] Translated

4. This letter has been:
   - [ ] Reflected
   - [ ] Rotated
   - [ ] Translated

5. This letter has been:
   - [ ] Reflected
   - [ ] Rotated
   - [ ] Translated

6. Draw the reflection of this shape.

7. _____ means moving a shape from its original position without changing its size, shape or orientation.

8. Rotate this shape $\frac{1}{4}$ turn clockwise around the centre point.

9. _____ is when a shape or line is turned around a centre point.

10. Translate this letter by moving it in the direction of the arrow.

Thursday

1. The order of rotational symmetry is ____.

2. The order of rotational symmetry is ____.

3. A triangle has a rotational symmetry of order 5.
   True [ ]   False [ ]

4. A square has 4 lines of symmetry.
   True [ ]   False [ ]

5. This triangle has been transformed by:
   - Rotation [ ]
   - Reflection [ ]
   - Translation [ ]

6. Draw the reflection of this letter.

7. Translate this letter in the direction of the arrow.

8. Rotate this shape $\frac{1}{4}$ turn clockwise around the centre point.

9. One of these letters does not have rotational symmetry. Ring it.

   O   X   I   K

10. Rotational symmetry is when a shape looks the same after it is rotated.
    True [ ]   False [ ]

Monday — Look Back

1. Continue the pattern.

   30, 36, 42, ____, ____, ____

2.

l	ml
6	345
+ 1	445

   _____

3.

k	g
2	106
+ 7	530

   _____

4. How many days in 3 weeks? ____

5. A rectangle always has ____ pairs of parallel lines.

6. There is an even chance of rolling an odd number on a 6-sided dice.

   True ☐   False ☐

7. 640 – 205 = _____

8. Name the 3-D shape of this net.

   _____

9. The order of rotational symmetry is

   _____ .

10.

Team Points

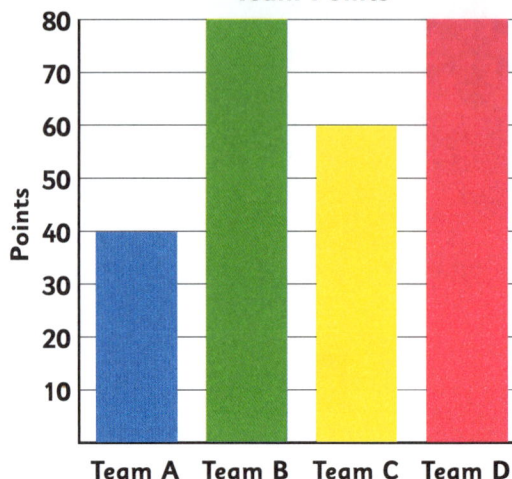

(a) Which team has the least points?

   _____

(b) Team C has ____ more points than Team A.

(c) How many points do the 4 teams have altogether? _____

Tuesday

1. Tessellating shapes are shapes that:

   ☐ Overlap
   ☐ Leave gaps
   ☐ Fit together without gaps or overlaps

2. A square can tessellate.

   True ☐   False ☐

3. Which one of these shapes can tessellate? Ring it.

   Circle   Triangle   Oval   Heart

4. Which one of these shapes will NOT tessellate? Ring it.

   Hexagon   Rectangle   Oval   Triangle

5. These triangles are making a tessellating pattern.

   True ☐   False ☐

6. Name the 2-D shape in this tessellating pattern.

   _____

7. Do these circles tessellate?

   Yes ☐   No ☐

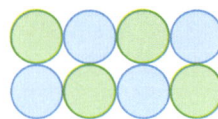

8. Why don't circles tessellate?

   ☐ They are too small.
   ☐ They have curved edges.
   ☐ They are pointy.
   ☐ They have corners.

9. Draw your own tessellating pattern.

10. This shape can tessellate.

    True ☐   False ☐

Wednesday

1. Is this a tessellation?
   Yes ☐   No ☐

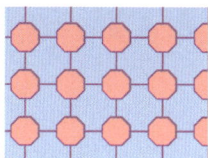

2. Colour the shapes that tessellate.

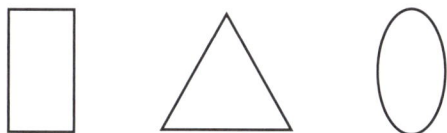

3. Which shape is used in a honeycomb tessellation? _____

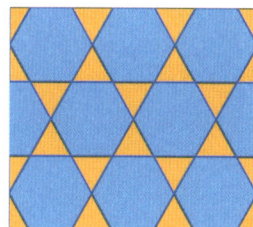

4. You can make a tessellation using just squares.   True ☐   False ☐

5. Draw a tessellation using only rectangles.

6. Name 2 everyday objects that show tessellation.
   _____ _____

7. Can a pattern of squares and triangles tessellate without gaps? _____

8. Which of the following shapes can be used together to make a tessellation?
   ☐ Squares and triangles
   ☐ Circles and ovals
   ☐ Stars and hearts
   ☐ Pentagons and circles

9. Which two shapes are used to make this tessellation?
   _____ _____

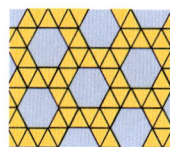

10. A semi-regular tessellation is made up of 2 or more polygons.
    True ☐   False ☐

Thursday

1. Continue this pattern on the dot grid.

2. What shape and colour is missing from this tessellating pattern? _____

3. What shape and colour is missing from this tessellating pattern?
   _____

4. Ring which of these irregular shapes can tessellate.
   (a)   (b)   (c)

5. Ring which of these regular shapes can tessellate.
   (a)   (b)   (c)

6. What kind of tessellation is this?
   ☐ Regular
   ☐ Semi-regular
   ☐ No tessellation

7. Can you make a tessellation using just a 5-pointed star shape? _____

8. Can you make a tessellation using just a 6-pointed star shape? _____

9. These tiles are a real-life example of irregular tessellation.
   True ☐   False ☐

10. A honeycomb is an example of a natural regular tessellation.
    True ☐   False ☐

Monday | Look Back

1. 56 ÷ 7 = _____

2. Rewrite these fractions from least to greatest value.

$\frac{5}{8}$ $\frac{3}{4}$ $\frac{1}{2}$ ⬜ ⬜ ⬜

3. One pencil case costs €4. How much do 5 pencil cases cost?
€_____

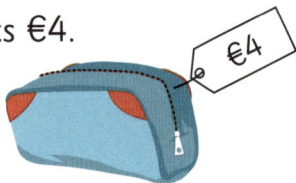

€4

4. What angle (right, acute or obtuse) is made by the time on these clocks?

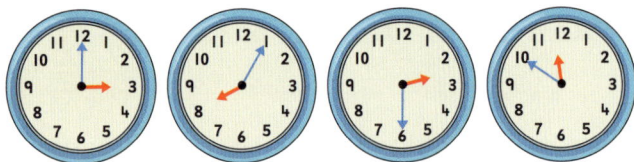

_____ _____ _____ _____

5. Write one hundred and twelve cents in euros and cents.
€_____

6. A jug holds 2 l of water. A glass holds 250 ml. How many glasses can be filled from the jug? _____

7. What time in the evening is shown on the clock?

_____

8. Leo's football training starts at 16:10 and lasts 1 hour 20 minutes. At what time does it finish? _____

9. Draw a count of 8 using tally marks.

10. What is the area of the coloured shape? _____ cm².

Tuesday

Continue the patterns and identify the pattern rule.

1. 23, 31, 39, 47, _____, _____, _____, _____, _____. Pattern rule: _____

2. 126, 117, 108, 99, _____, _____, _____, _____, _____.
Pattern rule: _____

3. 407, 417, 427, 437, _____, _____, _____, _____, _____.
Pattern rule: _____

4. 597, 593, 589, 585, _____, _____, _____, _____, _____.
Pattern rule: _____

5. 616, 621, 626, 631, _____, _____, _____, _____, _____.
Pattern rule: _____

6. 780, 760, 740, 720, _____, _____, _____, _____ _____.
Pattern rule: _____

7. 855, 845, 835, 825, _____, _____, _____, _____ _____.
Pattern rule: _____

8. 901, 908, 915, 922, _____, _____, _____, _____ _____.
Pattern rule: _____

9. 312, 309, 306, 303, _____, _____, _____, _____ _____.
Pattern rule: _____

10. 298, 263, 228, 193, _____, _____, _____, _____ _____.
Pattern rule: _____

Wednesday

Who am I? Write a numerical expression to solve these problems.

1. I am double the sum of 4 and 6.

   _____ = _____

2. I am the sum of 7 and 3 × 5.

   _____ = _____

3. I am the difference of 20 and 8, multiplied by 2.

   _____ = _____

4. I am the product of 6 and 4, plus 10.

   _____ = _____

5. I am 5 more than the product of 3 and 7.

   _____ = _____

6. I am the sum of 12 and 4, divided by 2.

   _____ = _____

7. I am the product of 9 × 2, minus 6.

   _____ = _____

8. I am 10 less than 5 × 8.

   _____ = _____

9. I am the product of 2 and 2, plus 12.

   _____ = _____

10. I am the sum of 5, 10 and 15. Then, I'm divided by 3.

    _____ = _____

Thursday

Find the value of the variable (w, y, z) to balance these equations.

1. $w + 5 = 15$

   w = _____

2. $20 - z = 14$

   z = _____

3. $30 + y = 45$

   y = _____

4. $z + 30 = 50$

   z = _____

5. $25 - w = 20$

   w = _____

6. $35 - z = 29$

   z = _____

w = ?

7. 🐷 + 🐷 + 🐷 = 9

   🐷 = ___

8. 🐑 + 🐑 − 3 = 7

   🐑 = ___

9. ⭐ ⭐ + ☀️ = 22

   ⭐ = 4

   ☀️ = ___

10. ⭐ × 🌙 = 24

    ⭐ = 4

    🌙 = ___

1.

🍎	|||| |||| ||||	
🍌	|||| |||| |||| |||| ||
🍊	|||| |||| |||

(a) How many apples were counted?

_____

(b) How many pieces of fruit were counted in total? _____

2. $56 \div 8 =$ _____ (R_____)

3. One notebook costs €1.75. How much would 4 notebooks cost? €_____

4. Liam has €20. He buys a book for €6.75. He gets €_____ change.

5. (a) How many days in a week? _____
   (b) How many days in a fortnight? _____

6. Round these decimal fractions to the nearest whole number.

   (a) 2.4 _____   (b) 6.7 _____

7. Write the time in the morning in 24-hour format.

8. 1 litre + $\frac{1}{2}$ litre = _____ ml

9. Noah went to sleep at 9:15 p.m. and woke up at 6:45 a.m. For how many hours and minutes did he sleep? _____ hrs _____ mins

10. Write these fractions as decimal fractions.

   (a) $\frac{3}{10}$ = _____   (b) $\frac{7}{10}$ = _____

Tuesday

1. Ava had 24 berries. She gave 6 to her friend and used the rest to make muffins. Each muffin had 3 berries. How many muffins could she make?

_____

2. Sam bought a gift costing €12 and a ball costing €3. He paid with a €20 note. He received €_____ change.

3. Mia has 5 boxes with 4 bracelets in each box. She makes 6 more bracelets and gives 3 of them to her sister. How many does Mia have now? _____

4. A book has 120 pages. Jack reads 25 pages on Monday and twice as many pages on Tuesday. How many pages does he have left to read? _____

5. Anna collects 10 stickers every day for 3 days. She gives $\frac{1}{2}$ to her sister. She has _____ left.

6. 25 people get on an empty bus at the first stop. At the next stop, 12 people get on and 10 people get off. How many are on the bus now? _____

7. Joe baked 24 pies. He packed them into bags of 6 and gave 2 bags to Joe. How many pies does he have left? _____

8. Sarah has €50. She buys a bag for €18, and flip-flops for €4 less than the bag. How much does she have left? € _____

9. A farmer has 5 hens. Each hen lays 4 eggs every day. How many eggs will the hens lay in 3 days? _____

10. 36 students are divided into 6 equal groups. Group 1 goes on a school trip. How many students are left at school? _____

Wednesday

1. Tom had 14 marbles. He won 12 more, gave 7 to his friend and lost 3. How many marbles does he have now? _____

2. Lucy bought a hat, scarf and gloves. What was her total spend? € _____

   €8 €4 €15

3. Oisín has 3 boxes of 10 crayons. He gives 9 crayons to Mae and 6 to his brother. How many does he have now? _____

4. The school play lasts 120 minutes. It starts at 3:15 p.m. and there is a 15-minute half-time break. At what time does the play finish? _____

5. There are 9 rows of chairs. Each row has 6 chairs. If 18 broken chairs are removed, how many are left? _____

6. James has 35 sweets and wants to give 6 sweets to each of his 5 friends. Does he have enough? _____ How many will be left for James? _____

7. Jane buys 3 packs of 4 notebooks and 3 more single notebooks. How many notebooks does she buy? _____

8. Alex had €100. He spent €35 on toys, €42 on clothes and received a refund of €10. How much money does he have? €_____

9. A baker made 48 cupcakes. He burned 10 and threw them away. 30 cupcakes were sold. How many are left? _____

10. Five shelves hold 8 books each. 17 old books are taken off the shelves and 9 new ones are added. How many books are on the shelves now? _____

Thursday

1. Bianca had €60. She spent €25 on a jacket and €18 on shoes. How much does she have left? €_____

2. A sports club has 4 teams of 7 players. 6 players leave and 2 players join. How many players are now in the club? _____

3. A pizza is cut into 12 slices. Ben eats 3 slices. His 2 friends eat 2 slices each. How many slices are left? _____

4. Zoe buys 6 pencils at 50c each and a pen for €1.20. How much change does she get from €10? €_____

5. A farmer has 7 crates of 7 apples. He sells 23 apples and gives away 7. How many are left? _____

6. Lily read 35 pages of her book on Monday, 28 on Tuesday and the final 12 pages on Friday. How many pages were in the book? _____

7. Mark earns €10 each week. He spends €3 and saves the rest. How much will he have saved after 3 weeks? _____

8. A classroom has 6 tables with 4 chairs. 5 old chairs are taken away and replaced with 3 new ones. How many chairs are there? _____

9. 54 counters are divided equally among 6 players in a game. In Round 1, Player 2 loses 3 counters. How many counters does Player 2 have now? _____

10. Sarah has €50. She buys a toy for €11 and another for €13. How much does she have now? €_____

Friday Week 1

1.
```
  h  t  u
     6  8
+    2  4
_____
```

2.
```
  h  t  u
  4  7  5
+    2  3
_____
```

3.
```
  h  t  u
  1  8  3
-    5  6
_____
```

4.
```
  h  t  u
  9  4  3
- 3  3  1
_____
```

5. How many hundreds (h), tens (t) and units (u) in each of these numbers?

(a) 327 = ___ h ___ t ___ u

(b) 506 = ___ h ___ t ___ u

(c) 851 = ___ h ___ t ___ u

6. Order these numbers from highest to lowest value.

645   936   748   102   360

_____ _____ _____ _____ _____

7. Order these numbers from lowest to highest value.

815   396   714   369   902

_____ _____ _____ _____ _____

8. Record these numbers in their expanded form.

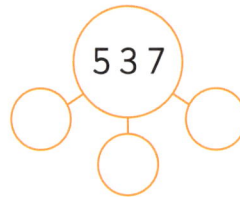

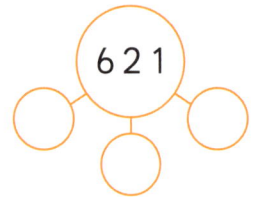

537   621

9. Show 507 on the abacus.

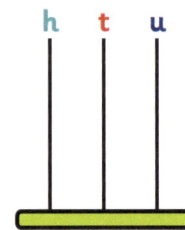

```
h   t   u
|   |   |
|   |   |
```

10. Problem-Solving

Saoirse rolled a dice 3 times and recorded the numbers 4, 6, 6. What is the smallest and the largest number you can make with the digits 4, 6, 6? _____ _____

Friday Week 2

1. 245 + 132 = _____
2. 648 − 327 = _____
3. 529 + 318 = _____
4. 807 − 469 = _____
5. A toy shop received a delivery of 356 brick sets. They already had 428 in stock. How many sets do they have now? _____

6. 294 + 157 = _____

7. 873 − 245 = _____

8. What is the sum of 376 and 429?

_____

9. 958 − 584 = _____

10. Problem-Solving

A farmer has 725 chickens. She buys another 189 and sells 342. How many chickens does she have now? _____

Friday Week 3

1. Complete the repeated addition sentence: $2 + 2 + 2 + 2 + 2 =$ _____

2. $6 \times 2 =$ _____

3. $3 \times 4 =$ _____

4. $5 \times 8 =$ _____

5. Write a multiplication sentence for 'Four times seven'.

_____

6. A farmer has 5 cows. Each cow has 4 legs. How many legs in total? _____

7. A bakery sells cookies in packs of 8. If Maria buys 3 packs, how many cookies will she have? _____

8. Write a word problem for 9×4.

_____

_____

9. Draw an array for the number 16.

10. Problem-Solving

Tom buys 3 packs of pencils. Each pack has 4 pencils. He then buys 2 packs of 8 pencils. How many pencils does he have in total? _____

Friday Week 4

1. (a) Continue this pattern.

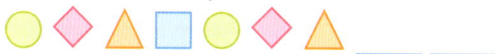

○ ◇ △ □ ○ ◇ △ _____ _____

_____ _____

(b) What is the rule for this pattern?

_____

2. (a) Continue this pattern.

□ △ ○ ■ □ △ ○ ■ _____ _____

(b) Rule:

_____

3. (a) Continue this pattern.

◇ ■ ◇ ■ ◇ ■ _____ _____

(b) Rule:

_____

4. (a) Continue this number pattern.

5, 12, 21, 32, _____, _____

(b) Rule: _____

5. Continue this number pattern.

100, 90, 80, 70, _____, _____, _____

6. $6 \times 4 = 24$, so $24 \div 4 =$ _____

7. $5 \times 9 = 45$, so $45 \div 5 =$ _____

8. $8 \times 7 = 56$, so $56 \div 7 =$ _____

9. $9 \times 7 = 63$, so $63 \div 9 =$ _____

10. Problem-Solving

Emily has 48 apples. She wants to pack them in boxes with 6 apples in each box. How many boxes does she need to pack all the apples? _____

Friday — Week 5

1. Subtract 2 repeatedly until you reach 0.

   16 ____ – ____ – ____ – ____ – ____ –

   ____ – ____ – ____

   How many times did you subtract? ____

2. Subtract 8 repeatedly until you reach 0.

   40 ____ – ____ – ____ – ____ – ____

   How many times did you subtract? ____

3. $18 \div 2 =$ ____

4. $24 \div 4 =$ ____

5. $80 \div 8 =$ ____

6. $28 \div 7 =$ ____

7. $12 \div 2 =$ ____

8. One box holds 8 muffins. How many boxes are needed for 64 muffins? ____

9. 20 pens are packed into boxes. Each box can hold 4 pens. How many boxes are there? ____

10. **Problem-Solving**

Lily has 48 beads. She wants to make bracelets.

(a) How many bracelets can she make if she uses only 2 beads per bracelet? ____

(b) How many bracelets can she make if she uses only 4 beads per bracelet? ____

(c) How many bracelets can she make if she uses only 8 beads per bracelet? ____

Friday — Week 6

1. (a) Continue this pattern.

   ◆ ◇ ■ ◆ ◇ ■ ◆ ◇ ■

   ◆ ◇ ■ ◆ ____ ____

   (b) Rule: _____

2. (a) Continue the number pattern.

   425, 430, 435, 440, ____, ____

   (b) Rule: _____

3. (a) Continue the number pattern.

   816, 812, 808, 804, ____, ____

   (b) Rule: _____

4. A sports club divides 48 players into 6 teams. Each team has ____ players.

5. Each week, Emily saves 5 coins. After ____ weeks, she saved 35 coins in total.

6. A farmer collects ____ eggs each day. He had 88 eggs after 8 days.

7. Ali puts 10 oranges in each box. There are 90 oranges in total so she will need ____ boxes.

8. One bus has 30 seats. How many buses are needed so 300 passengers get a seat? ____

9. 7 runners ran a total of 35 laps. Each runner ran an equal distance so each runner ran ____ laps.

10. **Problem-Solving**

Anna is knitting a scarf using a repeating pattern of red, blue and green stripes.

(a) What colour will the 24th stripe be? _____

(b) What colour will the 25th stripe be? _____

1. Ring $\frac{1}{2}$ of this set:

2. Write the missing fraction:

   $0, \frac{1}{4}, \frac{\square}{\square}, \frac{3}{4}, 1$

3. Write the missing fraction on the number line.

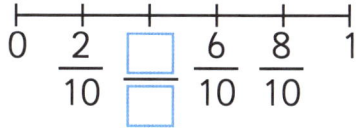

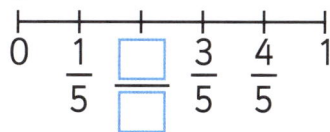

   $0 \quad \frac{2}{10} \quad \frac{\square}{\square} \quad \frac{6}{10} \quad \frac{8}{10} \quad 1$

4. $\frac{2}{4} = \frac{1}{2}$

   True ☐   False ☐

5. Write the shaded area as a fraction of the whole. $\frac{\square}{\square}$

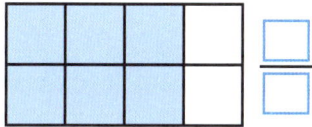

6. A pizza is cut into 4 equal slices. You eat 3 slices. What fraction is left? $\frac{\square}{\square}$

7. Which is greater: $\frac{1}{3}$ or $\frac{1}{6}$? $\frac{\square}{\square}$

8. Peter has 18 sweets. He gives $\frac{1}{3}$ of them to Ella. How many does he give to Ella? _____

9. Tadhg bakes a cake and cuts it into 8 equal slices. He eats 2 slices.

   (a) What fraction of the cake did Liam eat? $\frac{\square}{\square}$

   (b) What fraction of the cake is left? $\frac{\square}{\square}$

10. **Problem-Solving**

    Laoise has 24 cupcakes. She gives $\frac{1}{2}$ to her classmates, $\frac{1}{4}$ to her family and keeps the rest for herself. How many cupcakes does she keep? _____

1. Colour $\frac{5}{9}$ of the fraction wheel.

2. Use the correct symbol: <, > or =.

   $\frac{4}{9} \; \square \; \frac{2}{3}$

3. Write the missing fraction on the number line.

   $0 \quad \frac{1}{5} \quad \frac{\square}{\square} \quad \frac{3}{5} \quad \frac{4}{5} \quad 1$

4. Find the sum:

   $\frac{3}{9} + \frac{5}{9} = \frac{\square}{\square}$

5. Find the sum:

   $\frac{4}{10} + \frac{2}{10} + \frac{1}{10} = \frac{\square}{\square}$

6. Find the difference:

   $\frac{7}{10} - \frac{3}{10} = \frac{\square}{\square}$

7. Which is greater:

   $\frac{3}{5}$ or $\frac{4}{10}$? $\frac{\square}{\square}$

8. A farmer has 45 sheep. $\frac{1}{9}$ are black. How many are black? _____

9. A class of 30 students is divided into 5 equal groups. What fraction of the class is in each group? $\frac{\square}{\square}$

10. **Problem-Solving**

    Sarah has 90 beads. She uses $\frac{2}{9}$ to make bracelets and $\frac{3}{9}$ for necklaces. How many beads did she use in total? _____ How many are left? _____

Friday Week 9

1. $\frac{1}{2}$ m + $\frac{1}{2}$ m = ___ cm

2. Use a ruler to measure and record the length of this line.
   _____ ___ cm

3. Use a ruler to draw a line that's double the length of the line in question 2.

4. Fill in the correct symbol: <, = or >.
   2 m 15 cm ☐ 205 cm

5. Write in centimetres:
   5 m 18 cm = _____ cm

6. Write in metres and centimetres:
   505 cm = ___ m ____ cm

7. (a) Estimate the length of this pencil.
      ____ cm
   (b) Use a ruler to find its actual length.
      ____ cm

8. Calculate the total length:
   2 m 15 cm + 4 m 63 cm + 1 m 55 cm
   = ___ m ____ cm

9. Calculate the difference between these 2 lengths.

m	cm
8	52
− 4	73

10. **Problem-Solving**

    Evelyn, Olivia and Tomás decided to measure the lengths of some of their toys. Evelyn's train is 34 cm long, Olivia's toolbox is 56 cm long and Tomás's scooter is 95 cm long.

    (a) What is the total length of the 3 toys altogether? _____ cm; ___ m ____ cm

    (b) What is the difference in length between the longest toy and the shortest? ____ cm

Friday Week 10

1. This shape has an area of ____ cm².

2. Area of the smaller shape: ____ cm²

3. Area of the larger shape: ____ cm²

4. Area = ____ cm²

5. Area = ____ cm²

6. Area = ____ cm²

7. Area = ____ cm²

8. Show a shape with an area of 9 cm².

9. Find the total area of these two shapes.
   Area = ____ cm²

10. **Problem-Solving**

    What is the total area of the mixed vegetable patch, herbs patch and fruit bed?

    Area = ____ m²

    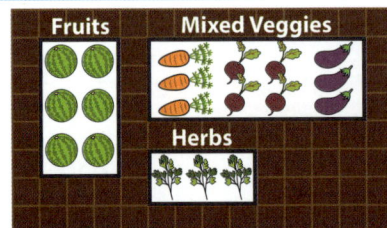

    Fruits   Mixed Veggies   Herbs

    Key:
    ■ = 1 m²

72 Assessments

1. (a) Colour $\frac{3}{10}$.

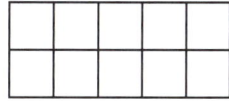

   (b) Write $\frac{3}{10}$ as a decimal fraction. _____

2. Write the number of raised fingers and thumbs as a decimal fraction. _____

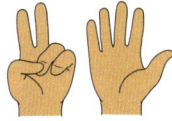

3. What decimal fraction of this shape is coloured? _____

4. What decimal fraction is coloured altogether? _____

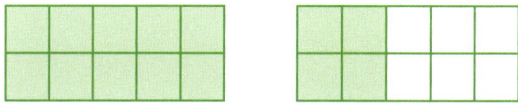

5. Colour 0.9 of this shape.

6. Colour 1.4 of these two shapes.

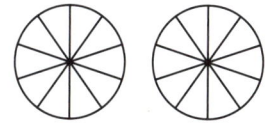

7. Colour 3.2 of these four shapes.

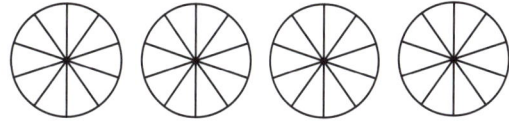

8. Ring the decimal fraction with the greatest value.

   1.3   2.1   4.6   3.3

9. Show these decimal fractions on the number line. 0.3, 0.8, 1.4, 1.7, 1.9

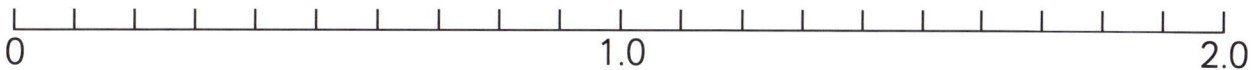

   0   1.0   2.0

10. Problem-Solving

   Sam cut 3 pieces of tape to wrap Zoe's present. The lengths of the 3 pieces were 4.2 cm, 7.1 cm and 4.7 cm. How much tape did Sam use in total? _____ cm

1. Round to the nearest whole number.
   (a) 16.1 → ____   (b) 23.6 → ____

2. Ring the number in which 7 has the lower value.

   11.7   17.4

3. Ring the number in which 9 has the lower value.

   19.5   11.9

4. Write the correct symbol: <, = or >.

   2.6 + 3.1 ☐ 4.2 + 2.7

5. 11.5 + 9.8 + 3.2 = _____

6. 19.2 − 6.8 = _____

7. Write these numbers in order, from least to greatest value.

   2.1   6.4   3.2   0.7   1.3   9.8   8.4

   ____ ____ ____ ____ ____ ____ ____

8. 0.5 = $\frac{5}{10}$

   True ☐   False ☐

9. 8.4 + 10.5 + 2.7 = _____

10. Problem-Solving

   Ríona jumped 2.3 m. Seán jumped 1.9 m. Zach jumped 2.1 m. What was the total distance jumped by all 3 athletes? _____ m

Favourite Hobbies

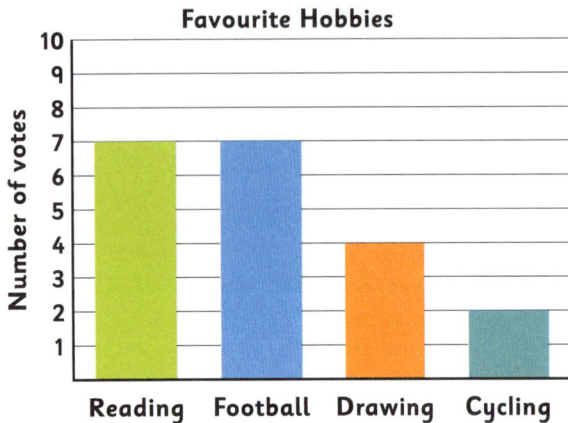

Bar chart: Reading 7, Football 7, Drawing 4, Cycling 2. Y-axis: Number of votes (1–10).

Favourite Zoo Animals

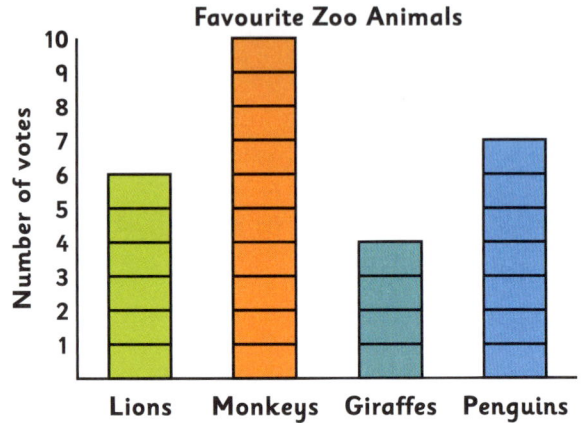

Bar chart: Lions 6, Monkeys 10, Giraffes 4, Penguins 7. Y-axis: Number of votes (1–10).

1. Which hobby is the least popular?

   _____

2. How many students like drawing and football combined? ____

3. How many more students like reading than cycling? ____

4. Which hobbies have equal votes?

   _____ _____

5. If 4 more students choose cycling, will it be more popular than football? ____

6. Which zoo animal is the most popular?

   _____

7. How many people like giraffes and penguins combined? ____

8. How many more people like monkeys than lions? ____

9. If 3 more people choose penguins, which 2 animals will have the same number of votes? _____ and

   _____

10. **Problem-Solving**

    This table shows the results of a whole school survey on favourite playground games.

    (a) Which game was the most popular? _____

    (b) How many pupils voted altogether? ____

Game	Votes
Tag	25
Hide and Seek	15
Skipping	50
Football	70

1. Draw a vertical line 4 cm long.
2. Ring the shape with curved sides.

   square   oval   rectangle

3. A hexagon has ____ straight sides.
4. Polygons have ____ curved sides.
5. Ring the smallest angle.

   acute   obtuse   right

6. A square has ____ right angles.
7. Perpendicular lines are straight lines that intersect at _____ angles.
8. A _____ has 4 sides of equal length and its opposite angles are equal.
9. A rhombus has all right angles.

   True ☐   False ☐

10. **Problem-Solving**

    A box of 2-D shapes has 3 squares, 7 rectangles, 4 circles and 4 hexagons. How many have no curved edges? ____

Friday Week 15

1. Convert these times to 24-hour format.
   (a) 3:15 p.m. ____:____
   (b) 7:40 a.m. ____:____

2. Convert these times to 12-hour format.
   (a) 15:30 ____:____
   (b) 23:05 ____:____

3. What time is it:
   (a) 5 mins before 2:20 p.m.? ____:____
   (b) 5 mins after 11:55 p.m.? ____:____

4. What time is it:
   (a) 5 minutes after 08:35? ____:____
   (b) 5 minutes before 18:00? ____:____

5. Write 10:05 a.m. and 22:15 in the same time format.

   ____:____   ____:____

6. Subtract 20 minutes from 8:10 p.m.
   ____:____ p.m.

7. What time is 45 mins after 5:25 p.m.? Give your answer in both formats.
   ____:____ p.m. and ____:____

8. What time is 1 hour 30 minutes after 3:10 a.m.? Give your answer in both formats. ____:____ a.m. and ____:____

9. Penny's swimming gala starts at 11:25 a.m. and ends at 2:10 p.m. How long does it last? ____ hrs ____ mins

10. Problem-Solving

Write a 30-minute time interval between 1:25 a.m. and 2:10 p.m.
____:____   and   ____:____

Friday Week 16

April						
Monday	Tuesday	Wednesday	Thursday	Friday	Saturday	Sunday
1	2	3	4	5	6	7
8	9	10	11	12	13	14
15	16	17	18	19	20	21
22	23	24	25	26	27	28
29	30					

1. How many Tuesdays are in April? ____
2. What day is the 25th April? _____
3. What date is the third Saturday in April? _____
4. What date is one week after 19th April? ____

5. How many Mondays are in April? ____
6. 1st May will be a:
   Monday ☐   Wednesday ☐

Bus	Departs	Arrives	From	To
201	8:15 a.m.	8:45 a.m.	Town	School
202	9:30 a.m.	10:00 a.m.	School	Library
203	11:00 a.m.	11:40 a.m.	Library	Park
204	1:00 p.m.	1:45 p.m.	Park	Town

7. Bus 202 leaves at ____:____
8. Bus 203 takes ____ mins to travel from the library to the park.
9. Which bus departs from the park at 1:00 p.m.? ____

10. Problem-Solving

On Monday, Saoirse takes Bus 201 from town to school. After school, she takes Bus 204 from the park back to town.

(a) How much time does Saoirse spend travelling by bus on Monday? ____ mins
(b) How much time is there between when Saoirse arrives at school and when she leaves the park? ____ hrs ____ mins

Friday Week 17

1. 6 × 5 = _____

2. A toy shop sells spinners in packs of 3. Mia buys 7 packs. How many spinners does she have? _____

3. A baker makes 6 cupcakes every hour. How many cupcakes will he make in 9 hours? _____

4. A mobile library has 7 shelves. Each shelf holds 5 books. How many books are there in total? _____

5. There are 4 tables in a classroom. Each table has 6 chairs. How many chairs are there in total? _____

6. 8 × 9 = _____

7. A train arrives at Central Station every 10 minutes. How many trains will arrive in one hour? _____

8. A farmer has 9 rows of crops. Each row has 6 plants. How many plants does he have in total? _____

9. A school has 5 classrooms. 7 students in each classroom are wearing a red jumper. How many students are wearing red jumpers? _____

10. Problem-Solving

Sophie is setting up chairs for a school assembly. There are 6 rows of 7 chairs.

(a) How many chairs are there in total? _____

(b) If 4 more chairs are added to each row, how many chairs will there be? _____

(c) After the assembly, Ben puts away 9 chairs. How many chairs are left? _____

Friday Week 18

1. 36 + 12 = 50 − 2

   True ☐   False ☐

2. Write the correct symbol to complete the equation: <, > or =.

   48 ☐ 6 × 8

3. Write × or ÷ to complete the equation.

   64 ☐ 16 = 4

4. Complete the equation.

   81 ÷ _____ = 9

5. 7 × 9 = 63

   True ☐   False ☐

6. Write the correct symbol to complete the equation: <, > or =.

   72 − 18 ☐ 40 + 14

7. Find the missing value: 55 + _____ = 88

8. Complete the equation.

   100 − _____ = 79

9. 9 × 8 = 72 − 9

   True ☐   False ☐

10. Problem-Solving

Lara needs 40 balloons for her mam's 40th birthday. Her aunt gives her 15 balloons. How many more does she need? Write your solution as an equation. _____

Friday | Week 19

1. Find the total amount of money.

   €____.____

2. You have two €2 coins, one €1 coin, and three 50c coins. How much money do you have? €____.____

3. €5 − €3.75 = €____.____

4. Dad buys a sandwich for €6.20 and a drink for €2.50. How much change did he get from €10? €____.____

5. €14.90 + €9.80 = €____.____

6. Sarah is saving for a new backpack that costs €38. She has €26 already. How much more does she need?

   €____.____

7. €50 − €21.50 = €____.____

8. A bicycle costs €45 and a scooter costs €37. The _____ is cheaper by €____.____

9. Two €20 notes + one €10 note = €60.

   True ☐   False ☐

10. **Problem-Solving**

    Jack buys a toy for €12.50 and a book for €8.50.

    (a) What is the total cost of both items? €____.____

    (b) How much change will he get from €50? €____.____

Friday | Week 20

1. Find the total amount of money.

   €____.____

2. €4.50 + €2.70 = €____.____

3. 50 − €29.90 = €____.____

4. Laoise's shopping costs €23.60. How much change from €50? €____.____

5. David has €40 and collects €8.90 at the bottle return bank. How much money does he have now? €____.____

6. Julie has €35. Her mam gives her €8.00 for doing chores. How much money does she have now? €____.____

7. Emily buys a pair of sunglasses for €38.20. She pays with a €50 note. How much change will she get?

   €____.____

8. Mark buys a football for €15.80 and a hat for €9.50. What is the total cost of both items? €____.____

9. Sarah buys a drink for €3.20 and a sandwich for €4.80. What is her total bill? €____.____

10. **Problem-Solving**

    Hannah buys a jacket for €38.50 and a pair of shoes for €45.00.

    (a) What is the total cost? €____.____

    (b) Hannah pays with two €50 notes. How much change will she get? €____.____

Friday Week 21

1. 60 ÷ 5 = ____   2. 90 ÷ 10 = ____

3. 35 ÷ 5 = ____   4. 27 ÷ 3 = ____

5. 72 ÷ 9 = ____

6. Amy wants to bake 24 cookies. Only 6 cookies can fit on one baking tray. How many trays will she need? ____

7. 42 ÷ 7 = ____

8. A teacher has 29 stickers and wants to give them out in packs of 4. How many packs can she make? How many stickers will be left over? ____ (R____)

9. A toy shop wants to display 31 teddy bears in rows of 5. How many full rows will there be? How many teddy bears will be left over? ____ (R____)

10. Problem-Solving

Hugh has 34 water balloons. He wants share them among 5 friends. How many balloons does each friend get? ____ How many are left over? ____

Friday Week 22

1. Write 'certain,' 'likely,' 'even chance,' 'unlikely,' or 'impossible' for each event.

   (a) A flipped coin will land on heads.

   _____

   (b) You will turn into a superhero tomorrow. _____

   (c) You will have a birthday this year.

   _____

2. What is the chance of rolling a standard dice and getting a number less than 5? _____

3. Which colour is the spinner most likely to land on?

   _____

4. Which colour is the spinner least likely to land on? _____

5. A bag has 1 yellow, 4 blue and 5 green marbles. What is the chance of picking a yellow marble at random?

   _____

6. A bag contains 10 blue tickets and 10 pink tickets. What is the chance of picking a pink ticket at random?

   _____

7. A lucky draw has 50 tickets for 45 small prizes and 5 big prizes. Is it more likely to win a small prize or a big prize? _____

8. A bag of sweets has 12 red, 6 blue and 2 green sweets. Which colour is least likely to be picked at random?

   _____

9. A spinner has 6 equal sections: 3 blue, 2 red, 1 yellow. What is the chance of landing on yellow? _____

10. Problem-Solving

Isha has a bag of 10 marbles. The colours are: 4 red, 3 blue, 2 green, 1 yellow

(a) Which colour is she most likely to pick at random? _____

(b) Ring the correct answer. Isha will pick a blue marble.

   certain   likely   even chance   unlikely   impossible

Friday | Week 23

1. What type of line goes straight across from left to right? Ring the correct answer.

   Vertical   Horizontal   Diagonal

2. Tick the pair of lines that are perpendicular.

   = ☐   + ☐   ✕ ☐

3. Draw an acute angle.

4. Match the angle to its name.

   obtuse angle

   right angle

   acute angle

5. Ring the larger angle.

6. How many right angles does this shape have? ____

7. A $\frac{1}{4}$ turn clockwise from west is south.

   True ☐   False ☐

8. A $\frac{1}{2}$ turn always points you in the opposite direction.

   True ☐   False ☐

9. Write the missing compass points.

10. **Problem-Solving**

    Ava walks in a straight line. She then takes a $\frac{1}{4}$ turn clockwise, followed by a 90° turn to the right. What type of turn did she make? Ring the correct answer.

    $\frac{1}{2}$ turn $\frac{1}{4}$ turn   full turn

Friday | Week 24

5	⚽		🍎	🚌	
4		🍐		☀️	
3				🌈	
2			🐕	🐦	
1	🎲			🌙	
	A	B	C	D	E

1. What symbol is at A1? _____
2. Where can you find the ⚽? _____
3. Where is the 🍎? _____
4. Which symbol is at E3? _____
5. Which symbol is at D2? _____
6. What is at B4? _____
7. Where can you find the 🚌? _____
8. Which row has the most symbols? ____
9. What is at E4? _____

10. **Problem-Solving**

    (a) If you want to visit the ⚽, then the 🌈, and finally the 🐕, write the order of the grid references you would visit. _____

    (b) How could you do it moving only right or down on the grid?

    _____

1. How many $\frac{1}{2}$ kg packets of rice are needed to total 2 kg? _____

2. Grace bought $\frac{1}{4}$ kg of 3 different cheeses for dessert. How much cheese does she have in total? _____

3. Tick the heaviest weight.
   $\frac{1}{4}$ kg ☐ $\frac{1}{2}$ kg ☐   1 kg ☐

4. Write the correct symbol: <, > or =.
   1,000 g ☐ 900 g

5. 3 kg 568g + 2 kg 255g = _____

6. 6 kg 850g – 2 kg 275g = _____

7. Róisín's package weighs 850 g. Tadhg's package weighs 950 g. Whose package is heavier? _____

8. Which 2 weights add up to 1 kg? Ring the correct answer.

   400 g and 600 g   250 g and 500 g

   300 g and 800 g

9. Tom's luggage weighs 4 kg 250 g. Anna's is 3 kg 750 g heavier. What is the total weight of both bags?

   _____

10. **Problem-Solving**

   Luca is buying some baking ingredients for the school bake sale.

   Luca's bag can only hold 4 kg. How many trips will he need to make to carry all the ingredients? _____

   Show your workings.

   Shopping list
   - 2 kg 500 g of flour
   - 1 kg 750 g of sugar
   - 3 kg 250 g of fruit

1. $\frac{1}{2}$ l = _____ ml

2. How much juice is in the jug? _____

3. Write the correct symbol: <, > or =.
   1 litre ☐ 900 ml

4. Ring the correct answer.
   500 ml + 250 ml =
   600 ml   750 ml   800 ml

5. Tick the greatest capacity.
   ☐ $\frac{1}{2}$ l   ☐ $\frac{3}{4}$ l   ☐ 1 l

6. 2 l 300 ml + 1 l 200 ml = _____

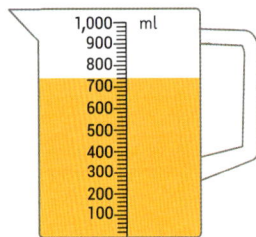

7. Charlie made a berry smoothie with 300 ml juice, 200 ml fruit puree and 200 ml yoghurt.
   What was the total quantity of smoothie? _____ ml

8. 3 l – 1 l 500 ml = _____

9. Zach had a carton of milk containing 1 l 800 ml. He poured 950 ml into a glass.
   How much milk was left in the carton?

   _____

10. **Problem-Solving**

   Lilly made a 1 litre pot of tea.
   (a) How many 250 ml cups can she fill from the pot? _____
   (b) Will there be any tea left over? _____

Friday Week 27

1. Complete the addition pattern.

    112, _____, 126, _____, _____, 147

2. Complete the number pattern.

    500, _____, _____, 425, _____, 375

3. Fill in the blanks.

    60, _____, _____, 240, _____, 360

4. I am a a multiple of 5 >, 40 and < 80. The sum of my digits is 11. ____

5. I am a 2-digit number. My digits add up to 7. My units digit is 3. What number am I? ____

6. I am a 2-digit number. My tens digit is 5. My digits add up to 8. What number am I? ____

7. ○○○○○○   ___ × ___ = ___
   ○○○○○○
   ○○○○○○   ___ × ___ = ___

8.
   triangle with 15, 3, 5

   _____ ÷ _____ = _____
   _____ ÷ _____ = _____

9.
   triangle with 63, 7, 9

   _____ ÷ _____ = _____
   _____ ÷ _____ = _____

10. Problem-Solving

(a) Fill in the missing numbers in Jen's 2 secret codes.

    60, 75, 90, ____, ____, 135

    200, 180, _____, 140, _____, 100

(b) Which number appears in both patterns? _____

(c) If Jen continues the first pattern, what will the number after 135 be? _____

Friday Week 28

1. Name the 3-D object with 6 square faces, 8 vertices and 12 edges. _____

2. Name the 3-D object with 1 circular face, 1 curved surface, 1 vertex. _____

3. Which 3-D object does this net make? _____

4. Name a 3-D object with 2 circular faces and no vertices.

    _____

5. Draw a cube and label:
   1 face, 1 edge, 1 vertex

6. This is the net of a _____.

7. Ring the odd one out.

    cube   sphere   cuboid   pyramid

8. Sort these 3-D objects into groups.

    cylinder   cone   cube   triangular prism

Curved Surfaces	Only Flat Faces

9. A triangular prism has:

    ___ faces   ___ edges   ___ vertices

10. Problem-Solving

Amir says 'A 3-D object with 2 circular faces must be a cone.' Do you agree? Explain your thinking and name any other object(s) that could fit this description.

_____

1. A ⬠ has _____ lines of symmetry.

2. Ring the asymmetrical image.

3. Complete to show reflective symmetry.

4. This letter has been

   A A
   ☐ reflected
   ☐ rotated
   ☐ translated

5. How many times will this star look the same in one full turn? _____

6. What is a star's order of rotational symmetry? _____

7. This shape has been

   P P
   ☐ reflected
   ☐ rotated
   ☐ translated

8. Draw the reflection of this shape.

9. Rotate this shape $\frac{1}{4}$ turn clockwise around the centre point. Draw it.

10. Problem-Solving

Alex draws a square. He reflects it over a vertical line and rotates it $\frac{1}{4}$ turn clockwise. Draw what you think it would look like.

---

1. Ring the correct answer. Tessellation describes shapes that:

   fit together with/without gaps or overlaps

2. Which of these shapes will NOT tessellate by itself?

   square   triangle   oval   hexagon

3. A regular hexagon can be used to make a tessellation.

   True ☐   False ☐

4. ◆ ◆ ◆   This shows tessellation. True ☐   False ☐

5. Which shape is used in a honeycomb tessellation? Ring the correct answer.

   circle   hexagon   triangle   rectangle

6. Can a tessellation be made using more than one shape?   Yes ☐   No ☐

7. This is an example of an irregular tessellation.
   True ☐   False ☐

8. Draw an example of a tessellation that uses more than one shape.

9. Name 2 real-life examples of tessellations. _____ _____

10. Problem-Solving

Ciara wants to tile her bathroom using 2 different shapes that fit perfectly together with no gaps or overlaps. Which 2 shapes could she use and why?

_____   _____

Friday | Week 31

1. 606, 612, 618, 624, _____, _____,

   _____, _____, _____.

   Pattern rule: _____

2. 750, 720, 690, 660, _____, _____,

   _____, _____, _____.

   Pattern rule: _____

3. 815, 810, 805, 800, _____, _____,

   _____, _____, _____.

   Pattern rule: _____

4. I am double 6 × 3. ____

5. I am the difference of 13 and 6, multiplied by 2. ____

6. I am the sum of 3, 6 and 9, divided by 3. ____

7. $y + 12 = 16$

   $y =$ _____

8. $18 - w = 9$

   $w =$ _____

9. $25 + z = 31$ $z =$ _____

10. Problem-Solving

Kate has invited 15 guests to her birthday party. She needs to buy enough cupcakes for everyone, plus herself. The cupcakes come in boxes of 6. How many boxes of cupcakes will she need to buy?

_____

Friday | Week 32

1. A baker made 56 buns. He sold 3 trays of 8 buns each in the morning and gave away 4 buns in the afternoon. How many buns are left? ____

2. Ella has €75. She buys 2 books costing €18 each. How much money does she have left? €____

3. There are 6 baskets of 9 oranges in the fruit shop. 15 oranges go bad. How many good oranges are left? ____

4. A video game costs €19. Jack buys 2 games and pays with a €50 note. How much change does he get? €____

5. A bus has 48 empty seats. 27 passengers get on at the first stop. 19 passengers board at the next stop. How many seats are now free?

   _____

6. Sophie has 72 purple beads. She needs 8 purple beads to make 1 bracelet.

   (a) How many bracelets can she make? ____

   (b) Will there be any purple beads left over? ____

7. Zoo A has 5 enclosures with 7 lions in each. 8 lions are moved to Zoo B. How many lions are left at Zoo A? ____

8. Leo collects 20 football cards every week. After 4 weeks, he gives 25 to his friend. How many cards does he have now? ____

9. Rachel has 36 cupcakes. She gives 2 boxes of 4 cupcakes to her aunt. How many cupcakes does she have left?

   _____

10. Problem-Solving

Tom's book has 80 pages. He reads 18 pages on Monday and 25 pages on Tuesday. How many pages does he still need to read? ____

100 Square

1	2	3	4	5	6	7	8	9	10
11	12	13	14	15	16	17	18	19	20
21	22	23	24	25	26	27	28	29	30
31	32	33	34	35	36	37	38	39	40
41	42	43	44	45	46	47	48	49	50
51	52	53	54	55	56	57	58	59	60
61	62	63	64	65	66	67	68	69	70
71	72	73	74	75	76	77	78	79	80
81	82	83	84	85	86	87	88	89	90
91	92	93	94	95	96	97	98	99	100

Multiplication Chart

×	1	2	3	4	5	6	7	8	9	10	11	12
1	1	2	3	4	5	6	7	8	9	10	11	12
2	2	4	6	8	10	12	14	16	18	20	22	24
3	3	6	9	12	15	18	21	24	27	30	33	36
4	4	8	12	16	20	24	28	32	36	40	44	48
5	5	10	15	20	25	30	35	40	45	50	55	60
6	6	12	18	24	30	36	42	48	54	60	66	72
7	7	14	21	28	35	42	49	56	63	70	77	84
8	8	16	24	32	40	48	56	64	72	80	88	96
9	9	18	27	36	45	54	63	72	81	90	99	108
10	10	20	30	40	50	60	70	80	90	100	110	120
11	11	22	33	44	55	66	77	88	99	110	121	132
12	12	24	36	48	60	72	84	96	108	120	132	144

Fraction Wall

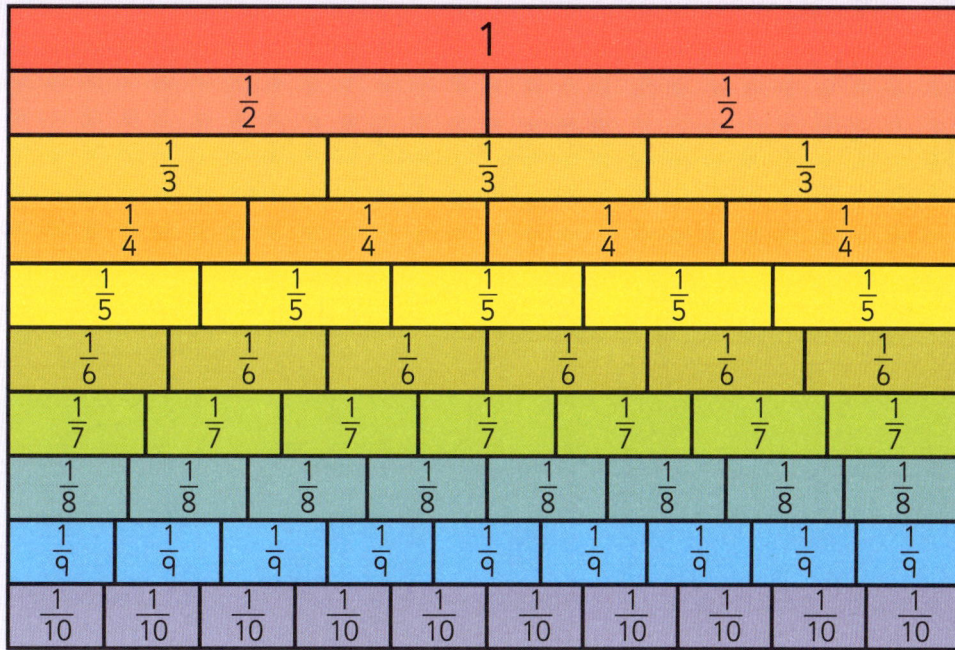

1									

$\frac{1}{2}$ · $\frac{1}{2}$

$\frac{1}{3}$ · $\frac{1}{3}$ · $\frac{1}{3}$

$\frac{1}{4}$ · $\frac{1}{4}$ · $\frac{1}{4}$ · $\frac{1}{4}$

$\frac{1}{5}$ · $\frac{1}{5}$ · $\frac{1}{5}$ · $\frac{1}{5}$ · $\frac{1}{5}$

$\frac{1}{6}$ · $\frac{1}{6}$ · $\frac{1}{6}$ · $\frac{1}{6}$ · $\frac{1}{6}$ · $\frac{1}{6}$

$\frac{1}{7}$ · $\frac{1}{7}$ · $\frac{1}{7}$ · $\frac{1}{7}$ · $\frac{1}{7}$ · $\frac{1}{7}$ · $\frac{1}{7}$

$\frac{1}{8}$ · $\frac{1}{8}$ · $\frac{1}{8}$ · $\frac{1}{8}$ · $\frac{1}{8}$ · $\frac{1}{8}$ · $\frac{1}{8}$ · $\frac{1}{8}$

$\frac{1}{9}$ · $\frac{1}{9}$ · $\frac{1}{9}$ · $\frac{1}{9}$ · $\frac{1}{9}$ · $\frac{1}{9}$ · $\frac{1}{9}$ · $\frac{1}{9}$ · $\frac{1}{9}$

$\frac{1}{10}$ · $\frac{1}{10}$ · $\frac{1}{10}$ · $\frac{1}{10}$ · $\frac{1}{10}$ · $\frac{1}{10}$ · $\frac{1}{10}$ · $\frac{1}{10}$ · $\frac{1}{10}$ · $\frac{1}{10}$

Multiplication Strategy Mat

Array

Skip counting

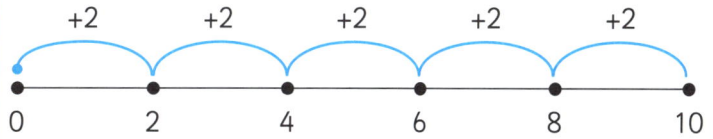

$+2$ $+2$ $+2$ $+2$ $+2$

0   2   4   6   8   10

Equal groups

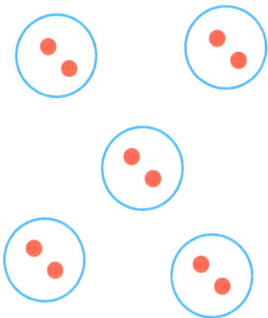

Olivia bought 5 pairs of socks. How many socks did she have altogether?

Repeated addition

$2 + 2 + 2 + 2 + 2 = 10$

Multiplication sentence

$5 \times 2 = 10$

Time

60 seconds = 1 minute   60 minutes = 1 hour

half past

quarter past

quarter to

five past

12-hour	24-hour
12:00 a.m.	00:00
1:00 a.m.	01:00
2:00 a.m.	02:00
3:00 a.m.	03:00
4:00 a.m.	04:00
5:00 a.m.	05:00
6:00 a.m.	06:00
7:00 a.m.	07:00
8:00 a.m.	08:00
9:00 a.m.	09:00
10:00 a.m.	10:00
11:00 a.m.	11:00
12:00 p.m.	12:00
1:00 p.m.	13:00
2:00 p.m.	14:00
3:00 p.m.	15:00
4:00 p.m.	16:00
5:00 p.m.	17:00
6:00 p.m.	18:00
7:00 p.m.	19:00
8:00 p.m.	20:00
9:00 p.m.	21:00
10:00 p.m.	22:00
11:00 p.m.	23:00

January
M T W T F S S
1 2 3 4 5 6 7
8 9 10 11 12 13 14
15 16 17 18 19 20 21
22 23 24 25 26 27 28
29 30 31

February
M T W T F S S
1 2 3 4
5 6 7 8 9 10 11
12 13 14 15 16 17 18
19 20 21 22 23 24 25
26 27 28

March
M T W T F S S
1 2 3 4
5 6 7 8 9 10 11
12 13 14 15 16 17 18
19 20 21 22 23 24 25
26 27 28 29 30 31

April
M T W T F S S
1
2 3 4 5 6 7 8
9 10 11 12 13 14 15
16 17 18 19 20 21 22
23 24 25 26 27 28 29
30

May
M T W T F S S
1 2 3 4 5 6
7 8 9 10 11 12 13
14 15 16 17 18 19 20
21 22 23 24 25 26 27
28 29 30 31

June
M T W T F S S
1 2 3
4 5 6 7 8 9 10
11 12 13 14 15 16 17
18 19 20 21 22 23 24
25 26 27 28 29 30

July
M T W T F S S
1
2 3 4 5 6 7 8
9 10 11 12 13 14 15
16 17 18 19 20 21 22
23 24 25 26 27 28 29
30 31

August
M T W T F S S
1 2 3 4 5
6 7 8 9 10 11 12
13 14 15 16 17 18 19
20 21 22 23 24 25 26
27 28 29 30 31

September
M T W T F S S
1 2
3 4 5 6 7 8 9
10 11 12 13 14 15 16
17 18 19 20 21 22 23
24 25 26 27 28 29 30

October
M T W T F S S
1 2 3 4 5 6 7
8 9 10 11 12 13 14
15 16 17 18 19 20 21
22 23 24 25 26 27 28
29 30 31

November
M T W T F S S
1 2 3 4
5 6 7 8 9 10 11
12 13 14 15 16 17 18
19 20 21 22 23 24 25
26 27 28 29 30

December
M T W T F S S
1 2
3 4 5 6 7 8 9
10 11 12 13 14 15 16
17 18 19 20 21 22 23
24 25 26 27 28 29 30
31

Spring	February
	March
	April
Summer	May
	June
	July
Autumn	August
	September
	October
Winter	November
	December
	January

Money

Conversion Chart

Volume	
100 centimetres (cm)	1 metre (m)
1,000 mililitres (ml)	1 litre (l)
1,000 grams (g)	1 kilogram (kg)

Less than <

Greater than >

Equal to =

2-D Shapes

A 2-D shape is a flat shape with only 2 dimensions.

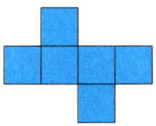 circle

semicircle

square

rectangle

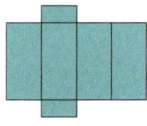 triangle

oval

hexagon

rhombus

3-D Objects

A 3-D object has 3 dimensions: length, width and height.

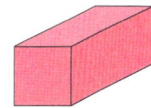

cube

cuboid

sphere

cone

pyramid

prism

cylinder

Shape Nets

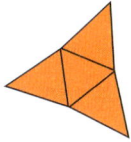

Cube

Cuboid

Square pyramid

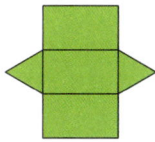

Cylinder

Triangular pyramid

Triangular prism

Transformation

Rotation

Reflection

Translation

Lines

Parallel lines are straight lines with an equal distance between them.

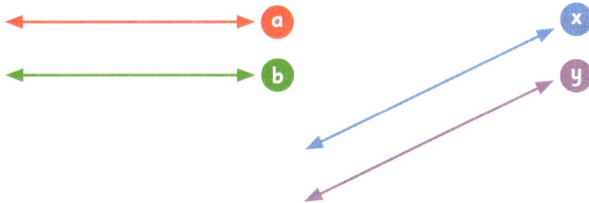

Perpendicular lines are straight lines that intersect at right angles.

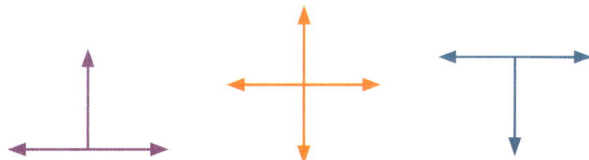

Angles

Right angle

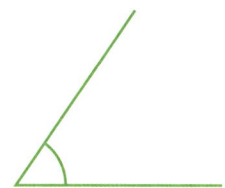

Acute angle

Obtuse angle

Maths Dictionary

Area: the area of a shape is the total size of its flat surface.

Array: a group of objects or numbers arranged in rows and columns.

Bar chart: a chart that uses bars to show information (data).

Block graph: a graph made of blocks to compare numbers or amounts.

Decimal fraction: a number with a decimal point to show parts of a whole.

Decimal point: the dot that separates whole numbers from parts (e.g. 3.5).

Denominator: the bottom number in a fraction. It shows how many parts the whole is divided into.

Divisor: a number by which another number is divided.

Dividend: the number being divided.

Edge: the lines that join vertices or faces of a shape.

Equation: a statement that two mathematical expressions are equal. Has an equals sign.

Even number: a number that can be shared evenly (a multiple of 2).

Expression: a combination of numbers, variables and operations that express a value. Does not contain an equals sign.

Face: any flat surface of a 3-D shape.

Fraction: a part of a whole.

Growing pattern: a pattern that increases or decreases by a constant unit.

Model: a system using mathematical concepts or language.

Numerator: the top number in a fraction that shows how many parts there are.

Odd number: a number that cannot be shared evenly.

Pictogram: a chart that uses pictures to show numbers or data.

Symmetrical: one half of an image is the exact same as the other half.

Tallies: marks used for counting, often in groups of 5.

Tessellation: a pattern of repeating shapes joined together without gaps or overlaps.

Transformation: a change to a shape, like rotating, reflecting or translating it.

Vertex/Corner: the point where two edges meet.